Diary of a
Drag
Queen

Diary of a
Drag
Queen

Daniel Harris

Carroll & Graf Publishers

New York

DIARY OF A DRAG QUEEN

Carroll & Graf Publishers
An Imprint of Avalon Publishing Group Inc.
245 West 17th Street
11th Floor
New York, NY 10011

AVALON
publishing group incorporated

Library of Congress Cataloging-in-Publication Data is available.

ISBN: 0-7867-1516-2

Printed in the United States of America
Interior design by Jamie McNeely
Distributed by Publishers Group West

Dedicated to the kind and unknowledgeable men and women at cosmetic counters around New York City

Introduction

I have never wanted to be a woman, and I do not want to be one even now that I am trying to be one. I never had any intention of saving my pennies and jetting off to Scandinavia for the so-called vaginoplasty and the tracheal shave (which reduces the size of the Adam's apple), never wanted to cut off anything more characteristic of my gender than the hair on my chest, nor to grow breasts more realistic than the padded D-cups of my dollar-store support bras. It is true that, as a child, I was famous among my peers for my impersonations of women, and it is also true that I have always been an effeminate male. And yet, appearances notwithstanding, I have never had any doubts about my manhood, never been plagued by gender confusion, never felt like "a woman trapped in a man's body" (although I *have* felt like a cute, petite, cuddly adolescent—alas, no corrective surgery yet exists—trapped inside the body of a brawny middle-aged giant).

It was something else altogether that drove me to drag—not a fetish for dresses but a fetish for pants and the heterosexual men who wear those pants. I am not a transvestite, someone who wears women's clothing all of my waking hours, nor even someone who dabbles in the art, a cross-dresser, as they say, but a shameless opportunist indulging in a fantasy rampant among gay men, that straight men are more authentically male than we are and therefore sexier, worthier of our adulation of their physical prowess and robust psychological health, which, along with their inaccessibility and contempt for homosexuals, have become, for far too many of us, ideal qualifications in a mate.

After gay liberation and the development of our political consciousness as an oppressed minority, it has become increasingly difficult to admit that one harbors this fantasy without opening oneself up to accusations (perfectly accurate ones, in fact) of being self-loathing, but since I have never claimed to be happy and well adjusted—healthy, normal, fully assimilated—I can afford to confess what large numbers of homosexuals feel but never tell, a dirty little secret that has been locked in the closet by a group otherwise committed to the politics of candor. I offer only this by way of self-exculpation: When one is taught from birth that gay men are morally reprehensible, diseased pariahs, child molesters, one may not want to select one's Prince Charming from abominations of the same ilk.

Drag for me has been a way of exploring this most common of gay obsessions. For my partners, in turn, it is a way of exploring one of the most common of *straight* obsessions, the heterosexual fascination with the hermaphrodite, the exotic she-male, who is at once alluring and forbidden, a creature that inspires lust and repulsion, fusing desire with that most potent of aphrodisiacs, transgression. In the bedroom of the drag queen, the heterosexual and the homosexual, like the lion and the lamb, lie down on the same sheets. It is a rare instance of the total concert of sexual desire among traditionally irreconcilable opponents. By fulfilling each other's contradictory fantasies, one fetish scratches the other fetish's back, theirs for the decadent, kohl-eyed transsexual slut, the false female, mine for the authentic male, the real McCoy, the ever-elusive heterosexual stud.

When I placed my first ad as a cross-dresser on Craig's List, a free online personals service, I was overwhelmed with an embarrassment of riches. Gorgeous men hailing from every country in the world came crawling out of all five boroughs of New York City, pounding on my door, baying disconsolately beneath my window, pleading for my charms ("Choose me, choose me!" one wrote), allowing me to experience just once in my life the rare thrill of being a haughty inamorata wooed by lovelorn suitors who showered her with poems, flowers, and compliments. I was soon to learn that poems, flowers, compliments—and very little sex— were all I was going to get, however, for while the fantasy of the exotic transvestite is widespread among straight men, a fantasy is what it usually remains, an unfulfilled erotic daydream that most men satisfy through a ritual that quickly became an irksome chore for me, the banal recital of obscenities during phone and cyber sex. Few men have the courage to act on their desires but hide behind their keyboards, using their mouse pads as mattresses, bedding beauties with foreplay so intense that repeated bouts transmit a new electronic STD, the chlamydia of the Internet, RMS, Repetitive Motion Syndrome.

As the initial promise of my first ads faded into the pedestrian reality of men who claimed to be twenty years younger, fifty pounds lighter, and three-by-four inches fatter and longer, something else altogether captured my interest: the disguise itself, which became almost a living thing, with its own vanity and its own devastating insecurities. My makeup bag quickly evolved from a tiny plastic zip-up pouch capable of holding some lipstick, a pot of cheap rouge, some foundation, and a liquid eyeliner to a shopping bag with fifteen shades of eye shadow, five foundations, six glosses, and four types of facial powder. It now contains approximately one hundred bottles, brushes, powders, gels, tubes, canisters, compacts, and jars. After I apply my toner, followed by my moisturizer, followed by my primer, followed by my beard cover, followed by my concealer, followed by my foundation, followed by my powder, followed by my MAC Fix-It spray, my makeup has so many geological strata that you could scratch your name in it. For my eyes alone, I use seven brushes, nine if you include the two I use for my eyebrows: an eyeliner brush to apply powders, an eyeliner brush to apply gels, a smudge brush to blur my eyeliner, a brush to apply my highlighter, a brush for my lids, an angled brush for detail work, and a blending brush, to say nothing of the brushes I use for my lips, the brush for my powder, and the brush for my rouge. I can now obliterate my eyebrows with Kryloan wax and spirit gum, erase five-o'clock shadow with red beard cover, conceal the dark circles beneath my eyes with a neutralizing yellow liquid, and snap taut the slack skin of my forehead with my "instant face-lift," an elastic band that, like an Inquisitorial instrument of torture, squeezes the skull so tightly that it can be worn for no longer than forty-five minutes before one nearly blacks out from migraine.

The pleasure of this transformation has become an end in itself even as my interest in my admirers has waned. Sitting down before my magnifying makeup mirror night after night, I feel like an actress preparing for an evening performance, an actress who suddenly realizes that the real drama occurs, not out onstage (in this case, on the boards of my bouncing box springs), but in the star's dressing room where the prima donna serves as her own best audience, peering at her image as she tickles her lips and eyes with feathery brushes, palpates her chin with a sponge reddened with Ben Nye theatrical cream, and taps her highlighter onto her cheekbones and down the bridge of her nose. In the months since I began doing drag, I have taught myself the rudiments of a science of the toilette, a highly technical discipline ill suited to a man whose morning routine once consisted of rolling out of bed and tousling the little that remained of his hair. I feel justifiably proud of all that I have learned because, although I have had my maternal muses, my mother surrogates, who have nurtured their homely daughter, an incompetent late-bloomer, through her apprenticeship as a female, I am by and large an autodidact when it comes to the tricks of grooming developed over generations. This ancient art of illusion is for some women so reflexive that they are unable to explain how or why they do what they do, much as a gymnast cannot explain the mechanics of a cartwheel or a ballerina the technicalities of a plié.

I can do all of these things and yet no matter how proficient I become, how adept at sculpting my face, how ingenious at raising a pert arch from the shapeless thickets of my scraggly brows, or how subtle in creating the plume of pigment that fans out from my Siamese eyes, I simply cannot make myself look like a woman. Someone could pack the entire line of MAC cosmetics onto my face, forming a thick impasto of pancake base and talcum powder, and slather on top half of Lancôme's products and pile on that a fragrant poultice made from the best of Chanel and yet the bulky, formless George Segal sculpture of a human being that remained beneath this hypoallergenic, antioxidizing carapace would still be identifiably male. My disguise has failed. Failed miserably. But something keeps me going, something I imagine that every woman who uses cosmetics feels, the conviction that somewhere out there, somewhere in some Home Depot of a makeup store, there is a panacea that will make her beautiful, a nostrum that will turn back the hands of time and liberate the vivacious young girl from within the dilapidated harridan with her flabby jowls and double chins. Like so many of my wayward sisters in this great sorority of cosmetic spendthrifts, I have become a slave to the beauty industry.

My diary is therefore at once the story of a sexual obsession, the class notes of a dutiful albeit singularly ungifted student failing her class on disguise, and also a voyage of rediscovery, the rediscovery of womanhood by someone who came to femininity the hard way, a route that all women once traveled but whose backbreaking exertions they may very well have forgotten. In addition to appealing to gay men, my natural audience, I hope to make readers of the gentler sex virgins again, take them back to puberty, to the first time they shaved their legs and bought perfume and learned how to walk in heels and fasten their bras by putting them on backward. I want them to reexperience the palsied lines of their first strokes of liquid liner, to make them suffer again the discomfort of rashes and razor burn, to relive the atrocious errors of taste they made during their first attempts at accessorizing and applying makeup, to feel again the embarrassment of those white-hot pants and that blazing splotch of Betty Boop blush. Mine are a fresh pair of eyes on the dilemmas of femininity. I know, far better than most, how hard it is to be a woman, having gone from pinafores to PMS in the space of a few arduous months.

My journey into womanhood occurred during an especially tumultuous period in my life, under circumstances that freed me from the constraints of my established identity as a writer and intellectual. A string of misfortunes—the loss of a boyfriend and two lifelong friends, along with a resurgence of the depression that has haunted me since childhood—left me doubting the viability of the old Daniel Harris who, tired of walking in his own shoes, decided to prance a mile in someone else's pumps. People who had known me for decades and who had developed certain expectations about my behavior (wearing women's lingerie was not among them) were suddenly absent and therefore could not question—indeed, mock—my inexplicable about-face, a defection into fetishism with no precedent in my past sexual history.

The fantasy of becoming someone else, living an alternative life, is seductive at the best of times, but is nearly irresistible at the worst, during crises in which others may change jobs, residences, or wives but in which I, perhaps because I lacked the courage to strike out in a whole new direction, chose to change—my clothes. For many years, my career as an author has been steadily declining, a seemingly irreversible trend toward insolvency paralleled by the dire straits of the publishing industry itself, which, to the misfortune of the mid-list author, is so misguidedly attempting to remake itself in the image of the large corporation. All three of my books have, to put a positive spin on it, sold *modestly*—so modestly in fact that, like the majority of writers lost on the shelves of Barnes & Noble, I am no longer very appealing to mainstream publishers. I approach middle age with no more security than my weekend job in a law firm as a word processor, a position I am both ashamed and dismayed to say I increasingly view as an affront to my dignity, now that it is apparent that it is not the temporary expedient I once thought would tide me over during lean times until I achieved success in my real vocation as a writer. In my mid-forties, I must somehow come to terms with the fact that the disciplined pursuit of my ambitions for over twenty years has resulted in nothing more challenging than a dull clerical career. Under the circumstances, the time seems ripe for an experiment in impersonation, a canceling out of a life that has reached its limits. Where does one turn when all of the routes of self-advancement are blocked but to the freedoms offered by a vivid imagination?

I transformed Daniel into "Denial" simply by swapping the *a* and *e* in my first name to create a nom de plume that I occasionally Frenchify into "Denaille," or Hellenize into "Danae," eliding the last two syllables to form the name of the mother of Perseus, the imprisoned beauty whom Zeus visited in a shower of coins, unlike my own less-than-Olympian visitors who are more likely to request money than to offer it. With them, I must settle for the less-glamorous name "Dani," a cute, ambiguously feminine diminutive that saves me from constantly explaining the elaborate meaning of "Denial," which is meant to suggest the denial of my gender, the denial of my old identity, and, in honor of my morbidly skeptical attitude toward the world, the denial of everything sacred under the sun.

Experimenting with a new identity, however, led me in circles. I ended where I began, with the snake swallowing its own tail. In some ways, I have never felt more myself than when I am in drag, more conscious of the truth than when I am lying. To erase oneself is to know oneself, to recognize one's boundaries, which are never more heavily patrolled by one's internal border guards than when one attempts illegally to cross them, eluding the customary surveillance of one's own eternally vigilant immigration and naturalization service.

Being a woman brought out the man in me. Every change I attempted to effect in my body was met by my body's unwillingness, indeed, inability, to change. Every endeavor to be feminine, docile, soft, was thwarted by a deep-seated need to be assertive, domineering, hard. My real self shows through my disguise as invariably as, after only a few hours, the shadow of my beard shows through my foundation.

An opportunist, quite unlike the sexual opportunist who preys on straight men, was one of the first aspects of Daniel to reemerge out of Denial. Writing my diary became a self-sustaining activity, a literary challenge, long after the sex became a burden, even an annoyance, what might be quite accurately described as an anticlimax in comparison with the joys of putting on my war paint and donning the ceremonial robes of an aging Jezebel. I would probably have dropped the whole project if it weren't for the fact that the disguise, the lie, had become so useful to the truth, to the writer, who exploited this improbable odyssey as material for psychological analysis, social commentary, humor, and self-revelation. Denial has become Daniel's instrument, his scalpel. She is not a drag queen, she is a method of investigation, the incognito I have assumed both to explore myself and to poke around an unfamiliar world, spying on its inhabitants even as I make love to them.

Another aspect of my original personality emerged from Denial's extracurricular affairs. Since I was a teenager, I have viewed myself as an intellectual and, like most intellectuals, have taken great pains to foist this view on others, adopting a sophisticated fake-patrician accent and a colorful, if occasionally recherché, vocabulary, precious echoes of which ripple through my prose style to this day. In denying my personality, however, I found myself reduced to a state of social nakedness, deprived of the usual ways of clueing others in to my real status, class, and level of education, much as a doctor would feel if he were forced to wear the uniform of a cop, or a truck driver the pinstripe suit of a businessman. It is hard to emanate power and self-confidence when one is wearing an outfit that one finds, quite frankly, ridiculous. My whole disguise is thus haunted by nostalgia for my familiar bookish self, for the man behind the mask, and I am surprised to find that an experiment in kinky sex has quickly become an experiment in democracy, with the playing field between an intellectual and his often blue-collar partners suddenly leveled in a way that I had never anticipated. I became the common man in becoming a common woman, and in many respects my diary is a record of my discomfort with this loss of status, of everything that defines me in the eyes of others, from the stacks of books I carry with me at all times to my professorial glasses to my arch sense of humor. At the same time, my diary is a tool with which I attempt to retrieve this status by placing anonymous sexual encounters in an analytical context that will allow me, on the page, if not on the bed, to reassert my rank, to correct, even after the fact, the mistaken impression that I am a brainless bimbo. I wrestle with issues of class in my diary, sometimes with more, sometimes less success, sometimes as a snob, sometimes as a sansculottist, a stuffed shirt, and a die-hard populist. Stripped of my social standing by my disguise, I re-create it with my prose, drawing on the artifice of another more familiar disguise, that of Daniel the artiste, the literary persona that has been my constant companion for well over twenty years.

The issue of class also arises frequently in my diary because gay sex is a profoundly classless experience, unlike straight sex which tends to occur among partners of the same education and income bracket. Heterosexuals view the old saw about love being the universal language as a romantic fabrication, idyllic if false, but the promiscuous gay man is actually fluent in this erotic Esperanto. He sleeps with men of all classes and his sex life resembles a Tocquevillean tour of America. Few lives are as eventless and internal as an intellectual's, its range extending no farther than a few feet, from the armchair to the bookshelf. Since I was a young man, sex has been a way of broadening my horizons, of introducing excitement and variety into this other-wise-sedentary existence, getting into bedrooms I would never have entered, meeting men I would never have talked to, jour-neying far afield from the groves of academe.

And now with the Internet, the intellectual can indulge his inertia and make this venture into the unknown without even leaving his house, his study—indeed, his desk chair. Online cruising provides atomized, agoraphobic misanthropes like myself with take-out sex. What's more, since I am in drag for at most four or five hours every day and will not leave my apartment wearing Denial's flimsy peekaboo raiment, I would never have been able to write this book were it not for the so-called "online community" which has saved me the embarrassment and inconvenience of running expensive personal ads, loitering in seedy bars, and taking my life in my hands commuting back to Brooklyn on the subway after an evening carousing in the fleshpots of the big city.

The Internet not only permits sedentary people to meet dozens of friends within minutes, it is tailor-made for disguises, for the preposterous misrepresentations alluded to in the by-now-famous *New Yorker* cartoon, which depicts a dog sitting at a terminal chat-ting away with prospective partners, an image the artist captioned with the words "on the Internet, no one knows you are a dog." Likewise, no one knows that, while I am not a dog per se, I am a bald, forty-six-year-old writer, that I am 6'2'' and 190 pounds, and that I wear size 14 heels. The Internet affords its users a luxury that large cities have provided for only a few centuries: anonymity, the opportunity to cut yourself free from the expecta-tions of your family and friends and re-create yourself on the clean slate of a stranger's mind. AOL, the Internet service that I, against my better judgment, subscribe to, gives each member seven dif-ferent screen names, seven different ways of presenting yourself to others, seven different masks, and it is not inconceivable that the truly adventurous Web surfer could be a welterweight boxer one day and a drag queen the next. In real life, if one were to go to work as a welterweight boxer one day and a drag queen the next, one's colleagues would ask embarrassing questions and the effect of the disguise would be ruined, as is not the case when one is dealing with perfect strangers who know you only in the way you choose to describe yourself, through the case you plead to them, through the bowdlerized autobiographies you permit them to read. The Internet is a realm in which fictions flourish, a world of rumors and lies, of pure exhilarating mendacity, one in which, as many journalists who have relied on the Web as a source of information have, to their peril, discovered, there are no fact checkers, pedantic sticklers for accuracy, lifesavers for reporters, scourges for drag queens.

And yet anonymity has taken an enormous toll on me psychologically and I find myself yearning for that long-gone Golden Age in which I met men eye-to-eye and face-to-face, rather than JPEG to JPEG, pixel to pixel. Online cruising provides a highly mediated form of contact in which one flirts through photography, a medium subject to grave distortions, the primary one being the passage of time, since people not uncommonly use computer files that have a distinct sepia tint, or, worse, that they have pilfered from x-rated Web sites. What's more, even when the photographs are recent and really do belong to the sender, no one ever looks like their pictures, and a matinee idol turns out to be the *New Yorker*'s dog.

In face-to-face encounters, rejection happens gently (insofar as rejection can ever be gentle). People simply walk to the other side of the room, avert their eyes, and move on to the next specimen on the meat rack, the next slab of beef. But on the Internet, because we exchange files, not glances, rejection is deferred until a moment of anguishing inconvenience, until the very instant the door opens and one looks down into the sad, pleading eyes of that schnauzer so piteously wagging its tail or, vice versa, when the door creaks eerily back on its hinges and the visitor finds himself in the presence of a real, live William Wegman, an arthritic mastiff in a rhinestone collar and a wig. The Internet may have created greater sexual abundance but it has done so by intensifying the experience of rejection a thousandfold in that, rather than ignoring someone we don't find attractive, we actually have to eject them from our apartment or, by the same token, tell our crestfallen hosts that they are hideous, that they should return to the kennel from whence they came, and that we must leave. We are all insecure about our bodies, but the Internet takes this insecurity to the next level, to the level of terror. When I cruise online as a drag queen, I relive issues of physical self-consciousness that I had largely resolved as a man. I am going through yet another adolescence just as I was finishing menopause, so self-conscious have I become about my appearance. My diary not only records Denial's discovery of a whole new world but a whole new medium of communication, one that, like cell phones, which are said to emit dangerous levels of microwave radiation, may be hazardous to your health.

Diary of a
Drag
Queen

Her

I remember the first time I did drag—not the sort of drag that I am doing now, but screeching, camp drag, fright drag, drag that expresses not the love of femininity, but the gay man's triumph over effeminate stereotypes, which he defies by caricaturing them, performing a hygienic subcultural ritual in which he distances himself from the mannerisms of the limp-wristed fag. On my thirty-seventh birthday, while I was living in San Francisco, my German friend Christoph decided that the time had come for my initiation into a game that he and his boyfriend had long played, and so as a present they bought for me, without my knowledge, all of the things I would need, a gauzy rose dress, a wig as large and unruly as an over-the-shoulder faux fox-fur, and an immense pair of low-heeled beige pumps, which they found in an Oakland shoestore catering to black women. I was terribly uncomfortable with the whole charade but it would have been impolite not to go through with it after they had taken such pains to dress me and so I reluctantly let them "do" my makeup, the "doing" consisting of little more than smearing on a cakey white foundation and then drawing on fat red lips as succulent as those of Ronald McDonald.

Christoph's makeup, while no more subtle than mine, was perfectly hilarious. By dredging his face in chalky white powder, he imitated the pallid complexion of that languishing Aryan maiden, Hannelore, the wife of the much-despised German Chancellor

Kohl, then suffering from a rare allergy to sunlight, which would eventually lead to her suicide. He was the perfect sanctimonious image of unsullied Nazi motherhood and an apt foil to my own impersonation of Faye Dunaway in *Mommie Dearest,* a character I assumed by adopting a lockjaw expression of repressed rage, the same dour, humorless look, oddly enough, that I would fruitlessly attempt to soften almost ten years later when I posed for photographs taken by my tricks. Try as I might, I have never been able to exorcize Joan Crawford from the haunted wreck of my face, but her unhappy ferocity still resides there, an inappropriate carryover of one form of drag into another, satire into seduction, an indication perhaps of my true feelings about this enterprise, about my inability to take it with the degree of seriousness necessary were I to carry it off with any conviction.

I remember something else about my experiences with drag both on my birthday and on one notable occasion months later when Christoph, this time dressed as a hooker, not Lady Goebbels, took me to the annual Castro Street block party on Halloween, a drunken bash in which heterosexual suburbanites, contemptuously referred to by the natives as the "lookey-loos," thronged the neighborhood to gawk at the drag queens. I myself was dressed as a civilian in male clothing, but Christoph was decked out in fishnets and a leather miniskirt that climbed as high as the crack of his ass. Overwhelmed by the bottleneck of people in the street, we slipped into a pizza joint that was serving beer and drank out of plastic cups while leaning against the wall. Standing near us was a handsome blond athlete, straight and drunk, a classical American beauty separated from his teammates who were no doubt still carousing outside, lost in the crowd. He could not stop staring at Christoph's legs but gaped at his ass and thighs, his eyes smoldering with lust, his mouth open, at one point even wiping the froth of cheap beer off of his wet lips with the back of his hand, a move that struck me as almost obscene in its naked carnality. This look has lingered in my memory to this day, as has the image of that gorgeous frat boy, a pornographic ideal of blond virility, who, along with other Ivy-League Übermenschen of his type, have provided me with the fatuous measure by which I have unfairly judged the shortcomings of my own paramours, who fortunately have not judged me by the same high standards.

Him

L et's take my most recent trick. He was a young man, in a do-
rag and impossibly low-slung jeans, around twenty or twenty-
one at the oldest, from the projects down the street, thin as a rail,
the kind of thinness that makes you think that one of his mother's
many economies was her grocery bill. He showed no shame about
living in one of the most notorious public-housing complexes in
the city and mentioned it almost as if it were a tony address, a
gated community with the amenities of a beautifully landscaped
park just across the street and convenient access to downtown
shopping. In this regard, he was admirably self-possessed, unlike
other men I have met from the complex who, when I asked them
where they lived, simply gestured vaguely in that direction, too
embarrassed to say anything more specific than "over there," a
location that included sites as diverse and uninhabitable as the
Gowanus Canal and the BQE. My trick, by contrast, appeared
entirely unaware of the disgrace of poverty, not because he had tri-
umphed over it, but because it had simply never crossed his mind
that he had any cause to feel humiliated, exhibiting a kind of inno-
cence about his low status that disarmed and touched me. And yet
he was clearly conscious of the class distinctions that separated us.
He had difficulty, for instance, pronouncing commonplace words
like "ask" and "recognize." This is because he wasn't really talking
to me so much as translating, paraphrasing the street slang he

used with his peers, efforts that made his speech stilted, as if he were trying to talk "proper," like a black Eliza Doolittle struggling to articulate all of her h's.

My books may have contributed to his discomfort. He, like virtually all of the men I meet, expressed amazement about the size of my collection which, although by no means immense, is larger than what most people see outside of public libraries. I find their surprise oddly gratifying. It seems to confer on me some of the respect I once thought I would command from others and that I have finally secured in an unexpected and roundabout way, through the awe of my sex partners, a far cry from the admiration I was long ago convinced I would receive from other writers and intellectuals. Standing in the middle of my living room, the boy from the housing project looked around at my shelves with the kind of reverence that someone in the Middle Ages might have expressed for an alchemist, full of a respect that made me feel, in some indeterminate way, powerful and yet, simultaneously, weak, ineffectual, utterly irrelevant, a figure of prestige if a hopeless anachronism.

He may very well have been more frightened of my books than my costume. He said he had never been with a tv before, although he had spoken to one once and, of course, had always had his "fantasies," as all of my tricks refer to their illicit urges, a confession that reveals all too clearly how licit and sanctioned these desires have become, a normal part of any straight man's repertoire of secret longings. Coming out of the mouth of an uneducated man, a self-professed high-school dropout, "fantasies" struck an incongruous note. He did not impress me as a sexual maverick and clearly took a kind of self-exonerating pleasure in jargon. Most of the men I meet resort to clinical labels like "fantasies," "desires," and "urges" to legitimize their behavior, the banality of this quasi-medical terminology somehow draining the activity it refers to of all of the dread associated with it and, it seems to me, much of its pleasure as well. One simply needs to christen a taboo with a psychological catchphrase, to give it an institutional endorsement, tuck it snugly under a rubric, and it becomes eligible for Oprahization, for earnest yet unashamed public confessions, and any twenty-year-old from the projects can discuss his dark impulses without blinking an eye, proud to be "in touch" with forbidden drives.

Our encounter was unremarkable, if satisfying, but it ended in a way that always dumbfounds me: with a request at the front door for a "loan" of five dollars—always the same amount, never more, never less, which is why it seems to me a symbolic number, neither inconsequential nor so exorbitant a sum that it would genuinely inconvenience me. Perhaps because my vanity is wounded, I always interpret these surprise last-minute requests as racial insults on the part of black and Hispanic men (they are almost always black or Hispanic) toward someone they dehumanize—even despise—as a privileged white girl, a desperate character who invites—even deserves—mercenary treatment. Of course, there is the more conventional argument that, by requesting that I tip them for their favors, they are buying an alibi for their temporary deviation into homosexuality. But it may be more (or less) complex than that. In fact, it may even be the exact opposite of a racial insult: an expression of intimacy, a byproduct of the compassion I have expressed for them in the course of the inevitable postcoital conversation, a recognition that I am financially better off than they and will gladly extend to them my charity now that I understand the dilemma of their poverty and sympathize with their troubles as members of downtrodden minorities. But however it is intended—however misinterpreted—it is always met with my flinging open the door, like an angel presiding over their expulsion from paradise, seething with rage, muttering the same cold, dismissive refusal followed immediately, without another word, by their crestfallen departure, at once ashamed and outraged that their virile performance couldn't even command chump change.

I am not emotionally equipped to be a woman. I am far too

impatient to sit back passively while men show off, especially when their performances are rarely entertaining. A case in point: a handsome twenty-two-year-old boy of Thai descent, who claimed he had never received a blow job and simply could not stop jabbering while I gave him one, all presumably to impress me with his cavalier sense of humor, with his "thuggishness," the by-now de rigueur impersonation on the part of suburban youth of inner-city ghetto "niccas," a performance that, in his case, lacked a necessary degree of conviction given that he professed to be the son of an affluent employee of the United Nations. At first, my need for sex and my attraction to his masculinity and good looks made me respectfully appreciative of his antics and I made an effort, however implausible, to giggle at the appropriate moments, something I can only hope I never witness myself doing because I am sure it would be quite frightening, tainted with both lust and an incompletely suppressed element of ferocity, a rage that probably made me look as girlish as a starving lioness stalking her prey. Perhaps he would have noticed, if the lights had been a little brighter, that my attentive expression of delight quickly congealed into impatience and that I sat frozen, unflinching, as he performed his galling routine of Young Hip Male. Maybe I am being disingenuous since I was the one, after all, sitting there in full regalia, performing a role for which I was hilariously miscast, an uncanny spectacle in my gauzy veils and transparent robes. I may not, however, have been the only one in the room in drag.

Last night I was expected once again to play dazzled female for a Sicilian construction worker who seriously misrepresented his physical condition, sending me ancient photographs, no doubt taken in his youth, of a handsome bodybuilder whose physique, some five years later, had disintegrated into a pasty blob. He was still handsome, however, and I was by and large willing to let him boss me around as he insisted on doing.

I found his use of the vernacular perplexing. In the middle of sex, he would look down at me and ask, apropos of nothing, "wattup wit chu?" And he responded to everything I said by feigning an idiocy that was supposed to be all shtick but that suited him more literally than I imagine he would have liked had he been able to watch himself in action. Every now and then, he would toss off a non sequitur that I believe was intended as a bon mot, "What happen?" now in response to my offer of a shower, now when I asked if I should call him a cab, a mannerism as unnerving as his insistence during sex of sticking out the tip of his tongue and wagging it frantically back and forth, all the while making obscene noises suggestive of a gluttonous binge.

He also hammed up the romantic element of the evening, asking me frequently why I didn't have a boyfriend and telling me that I was so beautiful, and how he couldn't believe that such a lovely girl, with such a beautiful figure ("figger"), would not have already been snatched up by some lucky guy, and how if he were my man, he would keep me locked up like a princess in a tower. No sooner would he lavish me with courtly compliments, however, than he would invent some imaginary source of conflict, as when I told him, having been asked, that I was really not interested in a relationship but liked playing the field, a statement that aroused intense jealousy which flared up as inexplicably as Othello's did of Desdemona. In my encounters with blue-collar men, I am always amazed by their sentimentality, by their adherence to the paradigms provided by TV and romantic comedies, the schools in which they have learned what emotion looks like, what one says when one is feeling anger, how one moves when one is feeling romantic, how to kiss, how to gesticulate with rage, how to deliver the words of the scripts they have been rehearsing all of their lives. The widespread belief that the proletarian is spontaneous, even innocent, is mistaken. There is no available sitcom prototype for casual sex, and the result is presumptuousness, a pretense that two perfect strangers are closer than they in fact are and that, far from having just met, they share a lengthy history that entitles them to insulting arguments, audacious demands for romantic commitment, and insolently smarmy forms of flirtation.

And yet it is also true that, while people tend to engage in bad theater when they meet to fuck, they can also be very candid, movingly so, about their troubles, revealing secrets that, under more genuinely intimate conditions, they would never even consider telling others, precisely because they know that the relationship seldom outlasts the duration of the initial meeting. How welcome it is to have a confessor, an innocent ear, someone to whom they can pour out their woes knowing full well that, although they may be judged, they will never have to see their judge's face again. The conditions for candor are ideal, if completely artificial.

During pillow talk, I become a dispenser of advice, the Dear Abby of drag, and my bed becomes a confessional in which men pour out weepy secrets about frigid wives, unfaithful girlfriends, wayward daughters, and drug-addicted sons, about jobs they detest and goals they have dishonorably abandoned in order to make money. I easily succumb to the narcissism and self-importance implicit in the role of oracle, and bask in their admiration, fancying myself the wise transvestite, a Solomon in fishnets and a lamé thong, a chimera, half whore, half sibyl. And yet not all of my advice is offered out of pride. I too am carried away by the intoxicating combination of intimacy and anonymity. I want to help these men in some way, want them to take home some consolation, if only the assurance that their fantasies are harmless and, besides, easily hidden. I try to offer them an impartial judgment, a disinterested point of view, on their dilemmas, presenting my neutrality as a gift in return for their company.

I have come to enjoy these moments of candor, albeit both brief and bogus. I have no social life to speak of and all of my human contact has narrowed to shallow encounters with neighbors and Hispanic grocery clerks with fake plastic talons and clownish circles of black lip liner. Under these circumstances, my nocturnal adventures have taken on an air of fiction, of fantasy, an Oriental lavishness, with each trick becoming an episode in my own *Thousand-and-One Nights,* a continually changing diorama of urban manhood. Not long ago I spent several hours with a funds manager who lived on Sutton Place; the next evening I was in the arms of a plumber, and the evening after I dallied with a Fire Department paramedic. Within the past few months, I have slept with an Italian journalist, a Hispanic teenager from Queens, a NYPD detective who investigates terrorist threats, a Jewish philosophy student attending Northwestern, a graphic artist for an advertising firm, a truck driver, a freelance copy editor, an architecture student at Pratt, a construction worker who specializes in concrete floors, an electrician, a vendor of tickets for local rock concerts, a supervisor at a research laboratory, a luggage inspector at an airport, a "male escort" who claimed to have read Housman and Yeats, a dispatcher for a cab company, and a mad Albanian who nearly kissed me when I mentioned that I had read and liked the novels of Ismail Kadare. The frightening vacuity of my personal life is filled with this parade of professions and types, a spectacle so varied and unpredictable that I am seldom aware of the extent of my solitude, of the barrenness and monotony of my isolation.

Her

I have never been a very resourceful person when it comes to
making friends, and yet in one special sense I am nothing less
than a social butterfly, the Paris Hilton of the bushes and the bathhouses, the hermit whore, a paradoxical creature who seeks relief
from her seclusion through fucking, not friendship. Only once
during my forty-six years have I had anything resembling a
normal social life, and this was through no fault of my own but
through my devilishly charming ex-boyfriend John, who came to
me as a kind of package deal, offering both his own companionship and that of his fiercely loyal friends, many of whom were so
protective of this gentle eccentric that they viewed me as a cynical
interloper, a tagalong who unfairly monopolized his affections.
For the five years I was with him, I led the charmed life of a gad-
about-town, if only as his escort, a parasite on his busy itinerary of
dinner parties, trips to the museum, and outings to the country.
When he left me unexpectedly two years ago, his friends went
with him, and my world instantly shrank back to the solipsistic
state to which I am accustomed. I was forced to settle for the
meager itinerary offered by another lover, an escort far less
charming, yet even more gregarious, as I have discovered, than
John: my computer, the new social secretary of the hermit-whore.

Out of necessity, I have lived a solitary life. As a writer and intellectual, I have often foolishly felt that I had no time to cultivate

friends, that I needed to devote every waking hour to my work. Unlike their straight counterparts, gay intellectuals have what amounts to an ethnic tool for relieving the isolation of the cork-lined room: sex. Promiscuity is characteristic of the subculture as a whole, but the gay intelligentsia uses whorishness to combat the monastic solitude of the life of the mind. Gay writers are almost as a rule of thumb libertines, fornicating alley cats whose study breaks consist of restorative jaunts to cruise parks and dirty-book stores where they find a temporary respite from their loneliness in the arms of perfect strangers. Denial may not look like an intellectual, but she remains one at heart and she conducts her private life exactly as the old Daniel did, alternating between intense sessions of reading and writing and furious bouts of fucking. Some might see my reclusiveness and my promiscuity as a contradiction in terms, but in fact the whore is sister to the hermit. The more I change, the more I remain the same.

Him

My new social secretary introduced me to quite a handsome man yesterday afternoon. I met (through AOL) a welder working on (it hardly seems a coincidence) the new AOL skyscraper at Columbus Circle, a project that, if one were to judge from the billboard at the site featuring two glitzy glass towers and a fancy high-rise atrium, looks Trumpish in conception, showy, ostentatiously expensive, with all of the piss-elegance of a Beverly Hills galleria. He, on the other hand, was no galleria—more of a strip mall, the very opposite of piss-elegant, rugged, handsome, tattooed with his wife's and children's names, disfigured by a long, thin scar that ran from his thigh to his ankle, an ugly red welt left when he was slashed by the ragged edge of a pipe, which virtually cut his leg in two. He was completely at ease with his own body as well as with mine and, at one point, simply laughed and picked off my ass a felt-tipped pen glued there by sweat, an accident I would have found momentarily embarrassing if he hadn't been so obviously amused. The only drawback to the encounter was his garlic-scented breath, which I succeeded in not smelling by keeping my nose well below the churning clouds that seemed to be swirling around his head and upper torso.

The sex was excellent and, even more gratifying, we had fabulous pillow talk afterward. He said he had been married for ten years and that during that time he had had sex with at least one hundred women and transsexuals, an average of one a month, a staggering record that any heterosexual philanderer would be proud of but that he, a modern Don Giovanni if there ever was one, mentioned in passing simply as a matter of fact. He told me that at home he was obliged to follow the fifteen-minute rule—i.e., he was expected to get his dirty business over and done with ASAP, a decree that he tried to follow so literally that his wife, whom he loved, had often been surprised and annoyed to catch him checking his watch during the act so that he wouldn't wear out her hospitality. He thought that she would take him to the cleaners if she ever found out that he was unfaithful, that he would lose everything, his motorcycle, his boat, his children (it was unclear if this was their order of importance), but he obviously couldn't help himself even though he recognized that his life was an accident waiting to happen, having had some of his extramarital trysts right in their master bedroom. More than once, he had had to look her in the eye and lie, now about the scent of a strange soap, now about a black scarf that one of his conquests had left in his SUV, an article of clothing that he had the audacity to claim was his wife's, having just dug it out from beneath the seat where he had assumed she had left it. There was something so refreshing about this man's guiltlessness, about his enjoyment of sex, about the sheer number of his conquests, which he mentioned without any macho bravado. He was like a heterosexual gay man in this sense, rapacious and willing to act on his impulses, a welcome contrast to most of the timorous men I meet online, who, at their lustiest and most aggressive, have sex with their keyboards, diddling with buttons, pointing and clicking at my digitalized charms, and then clicking and dragging me to the sofa.

Her

As the weeks go by, shopping for makeup and women's clothing inevitably becomes easier, so easy in fact that I sometimes feel as if I had sadly underestimated the degree of people's tolerance of aberrant behavior. Or perhaps Americans are more tolerant of drag queens than they are of the humdrum homosexual, the former being the staple of Hollywood films and therefore an endearing object of amused pity, the latter making a serious claim on their collective social and political conscience. What's more, I have only occasionally been candid about the real recipient of my compromising purchases. I throw caution to the winds in my increasingly frequent forays into the far-out world of the makeup counter, an epicene oasis which, up until this time, has remained terra incognita for me, put off as I've always been by the toxic clouds of perfume that hang in the air like smog around these glittering microcosms of exaggerated femininity. Caricatured eccentrics of the rarest breed still thrive behind those glass display cases, exotic sphinxes who exhaust their very limited powers of ingenuity on appearing aloof and girly boys in tight black sweaters and platform heels whose tastefulness presumably inspires confidence in the wrinkled dowagers who haunt these spas in search of the latest elixir of youth.

Not long ago, I made my first pilgrimage to the MAC counter at Macy's, a minute "boutique" crowded with a throng of hungry women, their hands extended like starving refugees at a camp kitchen where they beseeched the Red Cross cosmeticians for a little eye shadow, a smidgen of brow gel or bronzer, a lip gloss to save a dying child. They stood there three and four deep, milling about impatiently, craning their necks, their eyes fixed greedily on elegant pyramids of eye shadows and ziggurats of compacts and black velvet powder puffs.

It was my good fortune to be served by a dashing Trinidadian boy, muscular, attractive, sweetly effeminate, who gave me excellent advice, with no pretense whatsoever that it was intended for some imaginary sister or cousin, that someone other than the ghastly harridan before him was going to use that shimmer powder, wear that whorish blue eye shadow, or apply that liquid liner that promised to reshape my sunken sockets into slinky cat eyes. It was clear that I was not the first man to cross the perfume bar and enter this forbidden realm, although any man, no matter how "in touch" with his inner female, always feels like a pioneer in this sanctuary of feminine trade secrets. At this point in my experiment, it is impossible for me *not* to feel self-conscious when I shop for my alter ego, who causes me such embarrassment that, when I am running her errands, the god Machismo seems to be peering over my shoulder, full of Old Testament rage, ready to hurl his thunderbolts every time I thumb the nap of a teddy or atomize my wrist with a perfume sampler.

Among the many discoveries that I, as a man, have made about being a woman is how difficult it is to resist the beguilingly seductive packaging of feminine products. I have always felt smugly superior to the visual baits of advertising, but this is because the beauty products I am likely to buy—toothpaste, mouthwash, dental floss—are presented in drab cardboard boxes, functional dispensers, and stout plastic bottles, with little regard to their aesthetic appeal. My confidence in my immunity to the art of the store shelf is the result of inexperience, not of true understanding, since I have never really felt temptation, something that it is necessary to feel if one is to pride oneself on having resisted it. I am in a way a foolish, gullible virgin in respect to the snares of consumerism, the perfect dupe for the designers of jars of eye shadow that snap open like eighteenth-century snuffboxes and whimsically asymmetrical perfume bottles that seem to wobble and bend, perversely defying the conventions of the form. My certainty that I was somehow *above* the blandishments of advertising was founded on ignorance, for now that I am immersed in this realm of calculated exquisiteness, I need only look at a case of nail polishes in colors as brilliant as enameled jewelry or a counter equipped with sunken wells full of electric body paints and Day-Glo lip glosses to feel their siren call, their quiet tug on my wallet, and I will not leave the store until I have acquired something, anything, some superfluous cosmetic trinket that delights me with its precious, almost miniaturist appeal. I have fought a losing battle with depression all of my life, downing cocktails of psychotropics, antipsychotics, and mood stabilizers. A dozen psychiatrists and a small fortune in pills later, I find that I have begun self-medicating with lipstick and eyeliner— for many drag queens, the meds of last resort.

During only a few months of experimentation, I have spent at least $1,000 on my face alone, nearly one-twentieth of my annual income. This, of course, does not include the $2,000–$3,000 that I have squandered on clothing, jewelry, wigs, shoes, perfume, fake nails, depilatories, Lady Remingtons, waxes, and cortisone creams. All told, it is safe to conclude that I have spent approximately one-fifth of my salary on this project. Granted, I am an untrained shopper, and much of this money was wasted on mistakes that other women (note "other") would never have made: liquid foundations as white as the clown makeup of kabuki actors; roll-on highlighters as thick and pasty as spackle; dresses advertised as "one-size-fits-all" but that could more aptly be described as "one-size-fits-everybody-but-you"; and over-the-shoulder fishnet body stockings in which I have to strain and twist to wrench them up over my navel, let alone my nipples. I have never been more susceptible to consumerism than as a woman. It seems as if it is not only my appearance that I am changing but the gender of my economy as well, an arithmetical androgyne that would appear to have two separate sexes, one for the parsimonious writer starving in his garret, one for the spendthrift mall rat whose tight budget is collapsing under the expense of compulsive shopping sprees.

And it is not only that the products are prettier than those they make for men: They promise prettiness in those who buy them—a powerful combination of marketing magic that makes them all but irresistible, at once clamoring to be bought as precious artifacts in their own right—bathroom ornaments, hygienic tchotchkes—and as "beauty aids," snake oils for restoring one's dwindling youth and appeal. Presented like jewels in jewelry boxes, everything behind the cosmetics counter is exorbitantly expensive and yet everywhere one turns a great show of waste is made and the so-called "makeup artists" circle the customers powdering and slathering and spritzing with obscene prodigality. One does not see the same mad license in the local chain drugstore, where only the most foolhardy of employees would remove a product from the shelf, tear the lid off its box, and try it on the spot—thus violating a fundamental taboo of capitalism: that products are to be opened only after they are purchased. But then drugstores are self-service establishments, staffed by minimum-wage workers, while cosmetic counters are staffed by "experts," keepers of priceless treasures that cannot be left to their own devices out on the shelves, there to be mauled by the greasy mitts of careless customers who jumble the mocha browns with the brun pralines, the lash tints with the powder liners.

But Madison Avenue mojo will never make me pretty. Today I got back the photographs from the disposable camera I keep to document my progress with my makeup and look. They are, quite simply, appalling and I despair about all of the money I have wasted on lipsticks and highlighters, all the while believing that I was truly learning the art of disguise, that my face was becoming lovelier, younger, more radiant. And then to open the envelope and find this freshly exhumed corpse, teetering on spikes, moueing with geriatric lust, exhibiting my shapely legs like a poolside starlet from the '50s. Never has my face looked more haggard. The creases around my mouth, despite the concealer I trowel into them like a mason, look like culverts. The silver, shimmery powder I use to highlight my cheekbones appears metallic, inappropriately polished, like chrome hardware disfiguring a dilapidated antique quaintly covered with the dusty patina of time. The bags under my eyes make me look as ancient as a vampire, as if I had just sat upright in my coffin, famished, gaunt, cadaverously pale, ready to greet the dawn of a new night hunting for fresh blood. Only the most perverted fetishist could be enticed into the lair of this drunk, exhausted *fille de joie.*

To be fair to myself, the camera's flash destroys my disguise, takes a makeup job meant to be seen in dark, furtive corners and places it under a spotlight that would make any heavily made-up woman look like an escapee from the city morgue, Jane Doe, an unidentified suicide from drowning, caught by a grappling hook and dredged out of the Thames. When I "receive" my visitors, I turn on only one lamp, a moody, atmospheric rice-paper lantern that I have covered with my drawings and that emits a lascivious red glow of only 25 watts, a light so dim that men could indeed genuinely mistake me for a youthful thirty-seven, the stage age I use in my personal ads. The flashbulb, however, yanks back the curtain, exposes the fraud of all of my cosmetic voodoo, dispelling the illusion, like the famous photograph by Diane Arbus of the Coney Island fun house, which indiscreetly transforms the disquieting atmosphere of the attraction into something as sinister as a garage. But the fact remains that I am not beautiful, am not young, cannot be feminine, and that all of the king's horses and all of the king's men, armed with the complete arsenal of glues, sealants, and primers made by the best cosmetic companies, cannot caulk my face back together again. I began this project too late in the day to pull it off with the degree of success I could have were I truly thirty-seven—a thirty-seven, that is, that could withstand a bulb brighter than 25 watts.

And yet the rejuvenating effects of makeup and the fact that I am seen only while wearing lingerie are what make this enterprise so appealing. In the eyes of gay men, I am a menopausal failure, a flop, a balding, snaggle-toothed crone. And yet suddenly, at the age of forty-five, I am experiencing a sexual renaissance in which the men I fantasized about in my twenties, and who were far beyond my reach even then, are throwing themselves, if not at my feet, then at my thong-clad buttocks. The phoenix has risen from a bonfire of muscle shirts, Lycra gym trunks, and tight blue jeans wearing a wig, garters, and fishnets. I have repurchased my youth, not with monkey glands or cosmetic surgery, but with a few strategic acquisitions from Victoria's Secret, one of the most painless and, relatively speaking, inexpensive operations ever performed.

Long before John left me two years ago, it was clear to me that I had passed my prime and that, having seen the wrong side of forty, I could no longer compete on the open market of sex. Perhaps it would have been more sensible—certainly, prettier—had I accepted my fate at that moment and simply thrown in the towel, burrowing into my books, hibernating for the rest of my life, safe from the indignities of old age. Instead, at the very instant my confidence failed me, drag gave me a second wind and I reentered the fray for one last push before retirement, the last hurrah of a dying sex life. Drag for me has been a brief stay of execution, the gubernatorial pardon before my final shuffle in chains to the gallows of unglamorous maturity. Drag is about the loss of my youth, about the end of an affair at an inauspicious time in my life when my good looks, physique, and hair have all vanished, leaving me at the mercy of varicose veins and dimpled thighs, sagging buttocks, and bristly nose hairs. Women who are divorced late in life make a desperate bid to repurchase their physical appeal by going on diets and getting their hair done. Likewise, having experienced a painful divorce at the age of forty-four, I effected a more radical transformation in my appearance, one that has produced a windfall of unexpected sexual dividends at the very moment I was convinced I had run my last race.

The gay man's conventional response to menopause is to reposition himself as a "daddy" in search of "boys." My own response has been somewhat different: I have repositioned myself as a "mama" in search of "men." At first sight, the two strategies would appear to be diametrically opposed but on closer scrutiny, similarities emerge. Just as aging queens multiply their sexual chances by adopting the authoritative stance of pipe-smoking paterfamilias, so I have multiplied mine by adopting the wicked pose of the femme fatale. Who is to say which is the more effective technique of reversing the ravages of time? Both methods involve playacting, both a degree of dress-up. I have simply chosen the masquerade most in keeping with my sexual preferences as the passive partner, a bottom for whom the very idea of dandling younger lovers on my pederastic knee is ludicrous in the extreme.

I had been feeling slightly more confident, almost fully recovered from the blow of those ghastly photographs, when a series of online incidents left me more insecure about my appearance than I have been since I began seriously dressing in drag. After carefully (and very lightly) doctoring the heinous photographs with Photoshop in order to soften the glare of my metallic cheekbones and blur the creases around my mouth, I posted one or two of the much-improved images on the Web site I use for cruising. No sooner did I enter a chat room than one ill-mannered lout began taunting me about my ugliness, a refrain taken up by yet another boor, both of whom received some encouragement from the she-bitches in the room, who love the spectacle of a public stoning, having starred in such communal sports themselves, and who feel absolutely no esprit de corps, indeed who delight in the discomfiture of people they view as competition, contestants for limited resources. Before I knew it, my repulsiveness had become the topic of conversation, and I was being called Ozzy Osbourne and my look referred to as "very heavy metal," in reference no doubt to my admittedly heavy eyeliner and to the fact that my cheeks, despite the skin grafts of pink pixels I had pasted over them, were still as dazzling as fenders, not dewy so much as—tinny. I defended myself as best as I could, skewering them with my rapier wit until they lapsed into silence and I was able to retreat gracelessly from the battlefield, my self-esteem in tatters. Later, by pure coincidence, several men took it upon themselves to contact me simply in order to insult me again and inform me that "u ugly" and "u not even lok like a girrl."

I am still smarting from the humiliation. And yet I am fascinated that I should feel any humiliation at all. Denial, after all, is a prosthesis. She is not *me*. She is a decoy, a painted duck that mallards court, unable to discriminate between real feathers and the gaudy plumage of my camouflage. It is worrisome that I can be insulted by her humiliation. It suggests to me that I am truly becoming Denial, that I am merging with my alter ego, that I have more invested in her success than simply an abundance of sex and am no longer certain where I begin and my costume ends. I am acquiring vanity. Her beauty, her ugliness, is my own. It is not a pleasant prospect to become one's sex toy, one's puppet dildo, an identity that is encroaching on my much-compromised identity as a writer.

The transformation is especially unnerving when the dildo is so physically repellent. Since I wrote the last few paragraphs, I have received yet another series of photographs, this set taken by a walleyed black trick who came armed with a lot of patience and an extremely expensive digital camera. Unfortunately, the results of this photo session were even more traumatic than those of the last, for at least disposable cameras have the virtue of taking truly wretched photographs, indistinct and overexposed, whereas my trick's digital camera was unsparing in its clarity and detail. I felt so physically sickened after reviewing all of the files that he so generously sent to me only hours later that I poured myself a strong drink to settle my nerves and sank into my recliner, taking refuge in my novel, thinking all the while that I will never be able to go on with the project and that I should give up on sex altogether, returning to my ascetic life as the hermit intellectual. After I collected myself, however, I simply edited the files, snipped off all of the ugly pouting faces with huge, wet Fudgsicle lips and neon blue eyelids, and made myself a few perfectly acceptable photographs of my body.

What repelled me most about these images, quite apart from my wrinkles, puffiness, and general state of frumpishness, were the febrile swaths of rouge I had so ham-handedly misapplied, bright crimson splotches that looked as if they had been daubed on by a kindergartener finger-painting my face. Only the day before, I had gone out to Sephora and purchased a very pricey and, according to members of the cosmetic cognoscenti, very tasteful reddish, brownish, terra cotta-ish shade called "Plaisir" by Nars, which set me back some $20, $19 more than the sickly pink "twist-up" stick of Wet 'n' Wild I had been rolling on my cheeks like deodorant. My office mate Julie, one of my major sources of makeup tips, always mimes for me the proper methods of rouge application, kneading her cheeks and chanting "blend blend blend," advice I thought I had taken to heart, given that I jab and dab and poke and rub until my cheeks are so chafed that rouge seems scarcely necessary in light of the hectic flush I have raised through my own facial Rolfing. Unfortunately, one of the great drawbacks of my toilette is that I must put on my makeup without my glasses, and years of reading have left me virtually helpless without them, so that I doll myself up much as others paint by numbers, identifying the "Plaisir" spots marked "Cheeks" on a blurry anatomical illustration of my face and then trying to keep my brush from straying outside of the lines. I might as well be coloring myself with the help of Braille, so clueless am I about what

I am doing, an ineptitude exaggerated by the atmospheric lighting of my bathroom, which contains only one fixture covered with another of my hand-painted shades, lovely but useless.

If drag is my own equivalent of going on a diet after divorce and getting my hair done, my weight loss and new hairdo are not having the desired effect, and in fact I am beginning to feel that I would be much happier—and almost certainly more attractive—as a fat frump. The crisis of menopause that drag was intended to relieve has created the opposite crisis, the crisis of a belated puberty, which has given rise to a self-consciousness as harrowing as that experienced by any titless teenage girl with pimples and a retainer. My elixir of youth has had some unexpected side effects: It may have restored to me a modicum of the sexual appeal of my salad days, but it has also induced the glandular unrest of immaturity. Perhaps I would have been better off forgoing my gubernatorial, eleventh-hour pardon from lifelong celibacy and embracing my monastic destiny.

Him

Yesterday my visitor was a policeman in his thirties. He denied that he was a cop, but he wore an NYPD T-shirt and had COP writ large all over his face, the look of a former Bensonhurst delinquent civilized by the "sensitivity" curriculum offered at the academy. As with all of my tricks, I told him beforehand that I was a bottom and that I did not want—indeed, did not welcome— reciprocation, but naturally *his* desires prevailed and mine were ignored. He was desperate for dick and so I let him "do" me for five minutes but then broke away to remind him of the simple, reductive terms of the tryst—crudely put: you Tarzan, me Jane. He was clearly annoyed, but I was heartless and told him that I was not turned on, stopping just short of asking him to leave, hoping that he would be discerning enough to detect this unspoken invitation, which indeed he did but only after I had folded in on myself, my arms locking across my chest, my legs entwining themselves beneath me, like a flower closing all of its petals in preparation for the chilly night ahead. It is infuriating how men ignore the rules of engagement I always present to them when we meet online; no sooner do they enter the door than they flop themselves down on my sofa to be ravished or begin greedily to service me.

I find these men perplexing. They tell me that they could never suck a "real" man, that they detest hairiness, love softness, smoothness, femininity. They will never confess that they are gay, but they are quite open about their need for dick. In their company, I feel like a hermaphroditic prop whose physical presence reflects their deep internal conflicts. They hide their homosexuality from themselves by dressing up their cravings in lingerie, blocking out the male body with cloth, erasing my sex, creating a detachable penis, divorced from all that is male, thus minimizing the psychic damage of the experience. Rather than being interested in those who, as they say, "dress," they are really interested in those who *enshroud*, who mask, hiding the male body except for its equipment, which might as well be poking through a hole in a sheet. This is the type of trick I like least, not because I disapprove of their interest in dick, which, after all, I share, but because I feel I am being asked to participate in an act of self-deception, one that runs counter to my own interest in the whole farce, that of appealing to men as a *woman,* not as man mummified beyond recognition in ribbons and frills. So who is deceiving himself? The man who wants a man but only as a woman, or the man who wants a man to want him as a woman?

On the subject of the police, I am puzzled by the number of cops and firemen who are turned on by drag queens and am really at a loss to explain why the ranks of such conventionally macho professions should be filled with so many fetishists. Perhaps the policeman's obsession with transvestites is rooted in the conventional male's disturbed relations with women, who refuse to be as compliant, as demonstrably feminine, as the drag queen, a retro-slut who provides her testosterone-crazed admirers with a type of Stepford wife, someone whose old-fashioned girlishness complements their old-fashioned boyishness. In this sense, the uniformed male's romance with the trannie is simply a marriage of stereotypes, which find in each other's company relief from a world that is not as starkly black and white as the one they prefer to mate in but composed instead of a monotonous spectrum of sexless grays.

Perhaps also there is some truth to the stereotype that macho men are hiding doubts they have about their virility or, more plausibly, that the intimate, all-male conditions in which they work (the crowded cabs of fire trucks or the front seats of cruisers) create curiosity about the male body, a degree of polymorphousness resulting purely from friction, from the proximity of other men. What's more, their very safety, indeed, their very lives, depend on men behaving courageously, forcefully, dominantly, and hence they understand the importance—ultimately, the attraction—of masculinity in ways that perhaps even I don't—an attraction, however, that seems to be exclusively genital, since few cops or firemen make arrests or put out blazes in bulletproof teddies and waterproof stilettos. If this particular theory of their homosexuality were to stand up to scrutiny, uniformed men would have to be attracted to other traditionally masculine guys and not to someone like me who, although I can indeed, from certain unflattering angles (and most angles *are* unflattering), look like the driver of an oil rig, is not what immediately leaps to mind when one thinks of crime fighters ridding the world of terrorist kingpins and strapping heroes ferrying children to safety out of burning buildings.

It's also clear that cross-dressing has a particular fascination for the proletariat and that most cops and firemen are recruited from the working classes. Erotic taboos seem to be most strictly enforced among the middle and upper classes and blue-collar workers are more sexually experimental, just as they are, ironically, more homophobic and misogynistic. It is also true that some of the worst travesties of the unisex look occur among the lower classes, who wear leisure suits, sweatshirts, tennis shoes, and windbreakers—sexless articles of apparel designed for comfort and convenience, but as seductive as burlap bags. We live in a sartorially impaired world tyrannized by the androgynous dictates of informality. The prevalence of fat women with big hair and no makeup breeds fantasies of an altogether slinkier type of sizzling vixen—to wit, me—a femme fatale who restores sexual distinctions to clothing.

Her

B ig hair I may not have, but plastic hair is another story. I remember the first time I bought a wig. I did it on impulse. Otherwise I would never have found the courage for what amounted to a commando raid, a lightning strike on a shop with an inventory of some twenty or thirty ratty, shelf-worn carcasses tossed around the room like the smashed remains of high-fashion roadkill. I had just purchased a pair of heels at Payless Shoes and was a little high from the experience, it had been so painless and I had made such a wonderful purchase. I was on Fulton Street, the heart of the black shopping district, a low-budget Vanity Fair swarming with haughty teenagers striking insolent poses for each other, the girls strutting down the street seemingly unaware of the lewd homage the boys paid to their plunging cleavage, tight sweaters, and bulging behinds.

I was in a dangerous frame of mind. Once one begins to break taboos, it becomes almost a challenge to break the next and then the next, until one has broken so many that one feels like a terrorist of contemporary mores, so indifferent to the disapproval of the pack that it is almost a pleasure to insult it, to vandalize all of its sacred monuments. The fact that it was a young black shopping district and that I was surrounded by an atmosphere of frenzied teenage con-formity made me even more defiant than I would have been in a less tribal, more atomized, WASP neighborhood (where, incidentally, the shopping would have been much more expensive and, what's more, would have catered to more petite women whose lingerie, unlike the plus sizes so readily available in black districts, would have covered as much of my body as a postage stamp).

I stumbled on the shop by pure accident. It appeared before me like a mirage before a parched traveler. I seem to have conjured it up with my wishful thinking, and before I had a chance to turn and run, I heard the bell of the door jangling as I entered and— too late—felt the eyes of three clerks fall on me like a load of bricks. In fact, the weight of their stares was the result of my own paranoia because they were quite blasé about my appearance, which was anything but the sordid revelation that I imagined it to be. I forced myself to concentrate on the merchandise to the exclusion of all external distractions (the secret thus far of shopping for Denial, whose perverse errands demand rigorous philosophical detachment from the bustling activity of the shoppers in the immediate vicinity, an obliviousness to any hostile looks or disdainful smirks) and made my selection (an inappropriate one, as it turned out) with single-minded confidence and determination. I was treated with the utmost politeness, told how to tighten the wig, and then sent on my way feeling as if I had just slain a dragon, an heroic accomplishment almost epic in its danger and difficulty, indeed, its grandeur.

It was a $25 black number with auburn stripes that I had purchased for its stylized severity, thinking that, since I would never make a very plausible woman, I should attempt to create the impression of a glamorous androgyne who would seduce men by virtue of her flare for the uncanny rather than by the accuracy of her impersonation. In fact, however, the wig, in conjunction with my ghoulishly white face, made me look less tantalizing, indescribable, otherworldly than ferocious, almost ravenous, an evil spirit, a zombie—undead. It was clear that I needed to change this key element of my disguise if I were to deceive even the most gullible male and so back I went to the Fulton Street Mall where

I steeled my nerves and once again stormed a wig shop, this one run by an Asian woman in her sixties. I had called beforehand and asked if men could try on the wigs but apparently my request was misinterpreted—for when I arrived, the shop's proprietress kept foisting short wigs on me, pageboys and mannish bobs, as if I were seeking to hide my baldness rather than change my sex.

Buying wigs tests the mettle even of terrorists like myself. For one, there are no dressing rooms. For another, wig shops are not self-service stores in which one can try on any ready-made outfit off the rack without assistance. The owner usually presides over your "fittings," placing the wig on your head and then making a few graceful flicks at straggling locks with her pick as if she were a beautician putting the final touches on her "creation," stepping back and, with a swift rotation of the chair, pointing to the mirror as if to say "And voilà!"

What made this fitting especially grueling for a novice like myself is that the shop was in the back of a jewelry store run by surly Pakistanis whose eyes I felt burning holes in the back of my head as the dragon lady poked and fluffed and jabbed. After listening to her extol the virtues of a number of mangy shorthairs, I finally pointed to a ridiculous mane of distinctly feminine curls and said, "That one, I want to try that one." Any man would be paranoid in such a situation, and so one can never be certain of the reliability of one's reactions, but it seemed to me that there was a distinct pause as it finally occurred to her what I wanted. Her mouth rounded into a polite Asiatic "O" as she took the absurd brunette monster from its Styrofoam perch and slipped it on my head. Once the wig was in place, the little artistic jabs with her pick were somewhat slower and more dispirited than they had been, as if she were suddenly less proud of her creation, and there was an almost-imperceptible curl of her upper lip, an expression less of disgust than disbelief. I forced both her and myself to try on three more girly wigs, all the while feeling as if my face would burst into flames from the heat of blushing or that the Pakistani jewelers would at any second rush to intervene, rescuing the dragon from a situation as dangerous as a stickup. Fortunately, calm reigned, I waved the magic wand of my credit card and, followed by "Have a nice day" (directed, I'm sure, at American Express, not me), left the shop with my new identity in a brown plastic bag, a glamourless number that was nonetheless more feminine than the striped affair of my first spree.

My latest wig was perfectly serviceable, but was completely lacking in style. To add to its grandmotherly dowdiness, it quickly became matted with my face powder, so that the bangs looked coarse and grizzled, decidedly not the look of smoldering sensuality I was aiming to achieve. And so I decided that I needed to find an even bigger shop with a better selection than the moth-eaten specimens of the last two. I thus widened my search to Manhattan, where I found the perfect store, this one also run by Chinese women, who, along with Russian Jews, who cater to Orthodox women, apparently comprise the wig mafia of metropolitan New York.

I was immensely relieved to see that the door behind the counter leading to their storeroom was plastered with glamorous pinups of sultry drag queens, their lips slightly parted in breathless yearning, a sign surely that the proprietors were "drag friendly," to use the phrase designated for shops that welcome transvestites. Standing before the counter, moreover, was a whining virago, half man/half woman, a homeless creature in his late sixties, as ugly as a gorgon, pleading with the clerk to let him try on wigs without buying the $2.00 hairnet that the New York City Health Department requires shoppers to wear in order to curb the spread of lice. He simply would not accept the clerk's repeated explanations and his whine rose to a shriek as, at the top of his lungs, he asked the clerk, who beat a hasty retreat behind the counter, where she stood cringing as if she expected him at any second to leap over the case and lunge for her neck, "AND SO HOW AM I SUPPOSED TO HAVE SEX WITHOUT A

WIG?!!" "There but for the grace of God go I in twenty years," I thought to myself, unnerved by this chilling apparition of Christmases to come.

Once he was escorted out to the street by a fat Hispanic man who sold beauty supplies in the front of the store, she turned her attentions to me and, still somewhat frazzled, began searching high and low for a wig that would at once feminize my face and counterbalance the distinctly equine impression made by its excessive length, the homely genetic legacy of my dear Jewish father. She sat me before a mirror in a revolving barber's chair where I stared in amazement as she slipped over my head absurd mops of bouncing curls, now platinum blonde, now brunette, now a lurid carrot top, colors made all the more grotesque by the fact that they framed an unshaven, masculine mug which at that moment resembled nothing so much as Medusa's. Would that I could have turned to stone the sudden influx of customers who poured into the small shop, a noisy gaggle of Orthodox Jewish and black women, all of whom took one horrified look at the monster in the barber's chair and quickly averted their eyes in embarrassment—all, that is, save the six-year-old daughter of one of the black women who stared to her heart's content, too young (or too ill-mannered) to hide her curiosity. I felt like a cornered animal sitting in that chair, but I kept telling myself that this is just the way it is and has to be, that I must accept the consequences of my decisions, that I had nothing to fear except the unvoiced scorn of a handful of women I would never see again. Bucking up my courage, I forced myself to look into the eyes of the child and smile what must have been a psychotic leer, for the child's curiosity quickly changed to surprise and she grabbed the huge trunk of her mother's obese leg and peeked out from behind it, apparently assured that I could not grab her with my withered claws and devour her on the spot.

I have always been an iconoclast, sometimes without even trying but more often than not by dint of strenuous effort. When

I was nine or ten, I remember disliking the other kids in my rough, working-class school so intensely that I flouted the prevailing fifth-grade fashions and wore shoes as stylish as a farmer's brogues, an act of sartorial disobedience rewarded with many playground thrashings. I sought to make myself unacceptable to my peers, inviting exile, an ostracism surely as exhilarating as popularity, a banishment that made me feel alive, certain of who I was, circumscribed and defined by one harmless act of orthopedic rebellion. And now, decades later, I find myself up to mischief once again and perhaps for the same reason: to redraw the boundaries of a personality that has faded, to sharpen lines that have been erased, to make myself feel alive again simply by transgressing a sexual taboo. There was no doubt in my mind, as I sat in that chair exposed to the scrutiny of my fellow wig-wearers, who I was and what I was doing, who was right and who was wrong, just as I felt no uncertainty that my intolerant peers were behaving unjustly when they beat me up for wearing my clodhoppers, my earliest form of drag. An image comes to mind that has always represented for me the terrorist impulse. In a film by Margarethe von Trotta, a future member of the terrorist group Baader-Meinhof is shown at a high-school dance where, out of contempt for her priggish classmates, simpering in each other's arms, she takes to the floor by herself and waltzes around ecstatically, mocking their sexual conventionality. It is an innocuous image but, in its very sedateness, a surprisingly violent one, a convincing harbinger of what was to be an inglorious career of bombings, bank robberies, and kidnappings. Sometimes when I do drag, I convince myself that I am staging my own terrorist photo-op and that my obscene costumings express the same measure of contempt for my society that this girl felt, the same hatred for the status quo, the same urge to desecrate venerable distinctions between the sexes. And yet if I am a terrorist in a teddy, whom do I injure with the bombs I throw? Who feels the heat of my explosions? The men who come for the show? Who visit me precisely

because they are aroused by my careful, painstaking infringe-
ments of the rules of the game?

Thus far while shopping for the ever-greedier Denial, I have
made it a point to lie as seldom as possible. I feel that, if I am to
reap the sexual benefits of being a drag queen, I should experience the social discomforts of being one as well, a self-righteous
point of view perhaps but one that will give me greater insight into
transvestitism than if I took the cowardly route and pretended to
be shopping for my wife or girlfriend. I do not, of course, volunteer the information that I am shopping for myself (unless I am
talking to one of the sylphs behind the various cosmetic counters
I now frequent) but let the saleswomen make their own infer-
ences, as I'm sure they do even if, out of a discretion that can be
touchingly transparent, they refrain from inquiring about the
intended recipient of my purchases.

I have made only one exception to this rule. On a recent visit to
my family in North Carolina, my sister took me to a Goodwill thrift
shop as large as a department store where we combed through an
immense selection of lingerie. Once we chose something appropriate, Lynn would try it on in the dressing room, waiting for the
coast to clear and then opening the door a crack so that I could see
how it fit her, the assumption being that, if it didn't, then it would
never in a million years make it over my Amazonian shoulders. We
were naturally laughing hysterically about the whole absurd
adventure and Lynn, whose sense of humor can be as perverse as
mine, decided to tell the clerk, who had to unlock the cases con-
taining jewelry that we wanted to examine, that our many finds
were intended for "Aunt Betty," a big-boned woman with special
shopping needs, a giantess with wrists as fat as drainpipes and a
fire-hydrant neck that would instantly snap that fragile pendant on
the silver chain as delicate as a silk thread. Lynn persisted with the
joke until I, too, took it up and began referring to the strapping
Aunt Betty and her unpredictable tastes in accessories, much to the

DIARY OF A DRAG QUEEN

consternation of the clerk who hadn't a clue why we kept repeating our deformed relative's name and giving each other nudges and hammy stage winks. We left the store in stitches and sputtered with laughter the entire drive back to her house. Aunt Betty became our phantom relative for the rest of my stay in Asheville. This is the only time that I have deliberately deceived anyone about the real purpose of my purchases.

On the subject of my sisters, their response to my drag activities, insofar as they have had any reaction to them at all, has been extremely sweet and generous. Both raided their jewelry boxes to supply unwanted baubles to adorn Denial and both evinced not only a complete absence of shock but, more impressively, a complete absence of the need to demonstrate their tolerance. They immediately entered the spirit of the fun and began decorating me like a Christmas tree, festooning me with garlands of costume jewelry, throwing a family tree-trimming party that reached its climax when Lynn donated a blue mesh teddy that her boyfriend had given her in order to spice up their love life. After I returned to Brooklyn, I sent her photographs that various tricks had taken of me wearing the outfit, now on all fours, now leaning suggestively against my bookshelves, my hips exaggeratedly cocked to one side, like a scarlet lady lurking beneath a lamppost.

"So that's where that went," my sister's lover commented when Lynn proudly showed him the pictures.

It was my impression that terrorists were always at loggerheads with their society, but I find that my own immediate circle is not only unfazed but indeed amused by the bombs I am lobbing. It is pretentious of me to characterize myself as a terrorist in a teddy when the social milieu I inhabit is unthreatened by my mischief, to such a degree, in fact, that they make strategic donations of materiel of their own, not only of vulgar accessories that they themselves have long outgrown but of their expertise as cosmeticians and dermatologists. Where is the disapproval I should be feeling? Where the condemnation, the outrage? Polite society, it seems to me, is being all too polite.

Him

I am less likely to cause moral outrage than simple repulsion. Last night I met a black high-school dropout who lives just two blocks away. It was an odd encounter, first because he hadn't a clue, until I finally set straight, that I was a drag queen, even though he had seen and apparently appreciated my photographs online, and second because he was so insistent that I meet him that very instant, an impossibility given that I wasn't dressed and hadn't put on my makeup. At first he was puzzled that I was so vain about the way I looked that I refused to meet him unless I were fully made up and he began reasoning with me that I needn't be so sensitive about my appearance, that most women ventured outdoors with nothing on their faces but a little lipstick. He again demanded that we rendezvous on the street corner until I confused him even further by telling him that not only did I never appear unless I was done up to the nines but, once done, I never left my apartment and that, if he insisted, I would have to meet him as a man, a statement that, quite understandably, astonished him. Finally, he recovered from the surprise, accepted the fact that I was a man, and said that he would come over even if I weren't made up, asking only that I put on my wig and some stockings. Since this would spare me considerable inconvenience, I agreed, but made the unfortunate decision that I would protect him from the full horror of meeting a stubbly-faced witch by greeting him at the door wearing a veil, a black mesh shoulder harness that I had purchased from a store for Indian women.

Unfortunately, when he arrived and I poked my head out into the hallway, he visibly recoiled and said aloud "No!" as if he had seen a ghost or something even more frightening, as may very well have been the case. I closed the door but could see him lingering, indecisive, through the keyhole. I reopened the door and he approached again but when I displayed myself in all of my radiant splendor, this time without the veil, the dazzled mortal, blinded no doubt by my beauty, once more mumbled a panicked "No!" this time even more emphatically, and backed away, whereupon, insulted, I shut and locked the door, noisily sliding on the chain to demonstrate my fury. I then went back online, simmering with anger, to resume my cruising, whereupon, to my surprise, he sent me an instant message apologizing, saying that I had "scared" him, as he kept repeating like a little boy, that he had been frightened by my black outfit, my veil, and the "mad" (meaning excessive) perfume I was wearing. There was something rather touching about this immense, 6'5" black man, no doubt capable of striking terror in the hearts of many a little old white lady, to say nothing of many an adult white man, admitting that he was afraid of whatever it was that had greeted him at the door and so I agreed that he could return and that, as he insisted, I would this time dress as a man. After he left, very satisfied as he e-mailed me when he returned home, I thought to myself, "This is what I've come to after buying $25 powder puffs and $17 lip glosses. I am more attractive to straight men as a man than as a woman!"

Her

In perfecting Denial, seeing her through her untimely puberty, watching her anxiously, with both pride and despair—in large part, despair—as she matures into womanhood, I feel I am experiencing all of the self-consciousness of a pimply girl traumatized by her first period. I have slipped into my second adolescence, a harbinger of my second childhood, as apt a description as any of what has proven to be a supremely difficult menopause. Take, for instance, a recent encounter with an online acquaintance who claims quite plausibly, citing an impressive body of corroborating evidence, that he is—one of life's little jokes—a rectal surgeon, a resident at a local hospital who tells me he is in top physical form but whom I have yet to meet. On Saturday morning, a handsome Puerto Rican visited and we had fantastic sex even if he was not a very entertaining person but a morose, incommunicative gangbanger from the hood, on probation, or so he told me, for selling marijuana. Although we had satisfying sex (twice), it was clear that he thought I was ugly, as indeed I was, although no more so than usual, and refused to look me in the eye, reserving his attention for those parts of me that bore looking at, namely my meaty gams and tight calves exhibited to perfection in my five-inch fuck-me pumps. After we parted ways, I sent him a note thanking him for visiting me and, only hours later, received a note from him in turn, or so I thought, mistaking an e-mail from my surgeon for his. I then proceeded to tell the surgeon what a fantastic lay he was, how manly, how virile, a true gift to womankind, an expert swordsman, an Adonis, the usual fatuous compliments I lavish on my lovers. The surgeon, in turn, perhaps thinking that I was just flirting with him, began to dirty-talk back to me, calling me unspeakably filthy names that filled me with gratitude since they proved to me that my dealer had not found me ugly at all but was eager to experience once again a butt he described as "the bomb," adding that—music to a girl's ears—"I can't wait to rip that asshole up." All afternoon, we exchanged e-mails extolling each other's appearance and physical prowess until suddenly I remembered that he was the doctor, not the dealer, and that the delight I felt in the fact that I had at last pulled it off, that I had managed to excite an attractive man at least twenty years my junior, was based on a misunderstanding, and that, in all likelihood, my dealer had not indeed found my ass "the bomb" and would never return to "give me a good anal pounding" and, as he threatened, nay, as he promised, "treat me like a whore."

It was embarrassing that my eagerness to please had been exposed before a third party. What's more, the incident shows all too clearly that my interest in sex is not in experiencing sensual pleasure but in healing my own hopelessly wounded vanity. Having lost the game with gay men, I have taken on an even more insurmountable challenge, one that I cannot possibly win given my size and my age, to say nothing of my gender. It is as if having abandoned the trip up a grassy knoll in Prospect Park, I had decided to scale Mt. Everest instead, a test I am doomed to fail. I am intent, however, in enjoying some of the scenery along the way in what may very well be my libido's last stand.

I do not want to repeat myself here and dwell on my myriad humiliations, as is my wont, the name "Denial" being a reference, after all, not only to the denial of my gender but to my characteristic nihilism, my bleak and consistently black point of view on life, my habitual joylessness. Last night, however, I had another mortifying encounter with an attractive young man who came all the way from the farthest reaches of the Bronx to experience his first drag queen. Since it was late and my building locks the doors to the buzzers at 10:00 P.M. (an inconvenience with fascinating psychological consequences for my illicit recreations), I had to go down and greet him incognito, bundled up in a hooded sweatshirt, flannel pajamas, and—the crowning idiocy—a pair of glamorous black shades. God knows what he must have thought when he saw this overdressed clown on stilts hurtling, rather unsteadily, toward the door. He entered the building none-too-happily, it seemed to me, an impression reinforced by our uncomfortable ride up the elevator during which he stared straight ahead as if someone had a gun jammed in the flat of his back. I told him, not very convincingly I'm afraid (since I myself was not in the least convinced), "Don't worry, I'll look prettier when I get out of all of this stuff," but his sole response was "You're awfully tall for a girl," to which I responded (wittily, I thought) "I'll look a lot shorter when I'm down on my knees." He didn't even crack a smile and the rest of our conversation for the duration of the evening—all one hundred words of it—scarcely merits repeating.

The disadvantage of my height never even crossed my mind when I began dressing for sex, but it has emerged as major problem. It is one of the final questions—often the deciding one—that my tricks ask me when they can't make up their minds if they want to meet. Men are accustomed to their sex partners being considerably shorter than they are, and my height only increases the threatening nature of what is already an adventure fraught with anxiety, especially since I am not only 6'2" but 6'7" when I am wearing my favorite stilettos, which have 5" heels that make me look positively cloud-capped.

Once we were in the apartment, the situation did not improve, for he continued to look everywhere but at me—around me, above me, below me, through me, but never directly *at* me—an indication, if I am not mistaken, that he did not want to see any too clearly The Thing curled up in a provocatively feminine pose by his side, drawing feathery figure-eights with its index finger on the scruff of his neck. After a good thirty seconds of chitchat, he leapt to his feet and whipped out a condom, obviously hoping to end the ordeal as fast as possible, perhaps because he could see no acceptable escape from the apartment, as well as from the stranglehold of propriety that held him there, other than that most decisive of conclusions, an orgasm. Sure enough, after he came, he scrambled into his underwear, dressed hurriedly in the living room, and informed me that he would be right back, that he was going to the store for cigarettes and did I want anything (a question that, in retrospect, strikes me as almost insolent in its facetiousness)? Since I had heard the "store" excuse before (once I had forgotten to remove my reading glasses and had met a trick at the door in them, a harrowing sight of a homely bluestocking, which had sent my suitor packing as soon as he stepped across the threshold), I knew he wouldn't return and later e-mailed him that, come to think of it, I could indeed use a quart of milk and a dozen eggs, and would he please put a wiggle on it and hurry back.

I was naturally depressed when he left. How much brutalizing, after all, can one ego take and, what's more, wasn't there something morally wrong about enticing men over when I know that I could easily inflict irreparable damage on the innocent male retina, causing loss of vision or even blindness? I experienced profound misgivings about the whole project and thought to myself in despair that I will never make it, that the book that was helping to restore a sense of purpose to my life, after my three previous books, would never get written and that I would return to the procrastination and indecisiveness that had made me so intensely miserable in the last year. I poured myself another strong drink and sat down at the computer to cruise again, to see if it were true, if I really were as hideous as he had made me feel, indulging in a destructive game that led me to seek security and confidence in the very activity that had made me so apprehensive and self-doubting in the first place. How troubling that I have begun to contend with "self-esteem issues," as they say, that pertain to a body, a self, that isn't even mine!

As an atheist I am troubled by the evidence of religious extremism in my personality. Why, after all, would I willingly submit to this torture if it weren't for the conviction that it is somehow wholesome for me to feel pain, that it builds character, that the experience of being the ultimate ugly girl, shunned by her society, a pariah among women, will strengthen my moral fabric by bringing me face to face with the hostility of the crowd? Ugliness is indeed a form of saintliness for me, and I reward myself for it just as an anorexic rewards herself for starvation. Granted, writing this book has become an amusing organizational activity in itself, but I could always walk away from it. Nothing binds me to this project—no contract, no advance—and yet I continue to stretch myself on the rack, to expose myself to the ridicule of my tricks, to test my limits. I tell myself that if I can survive this ordeal by unsightliness, this martyrdom of self-disfiguration, I will become fearless, indifferent to the opinions of others, but isn't there also a danger that, as the object of constant derision, I will become, quite simply, as ugly as my detractors make me out to be? My self-righteous desire to fortify myself against public opinion by provoking its wrath may backfire and I may succumb to the constant mockery of Denial's homeliness, my moral fabric fraying under the strain, the calluses I had hoped to build becoming scars, hideous welts deforming my personality. Beauty and truth, beauty and goodness, have been linked throughout human history, but with the rise of otherworldly religions contemptuous of the flesh, so have ugliness and truth, ugliness and goodness. My martyr complex reveals a mystical strain in my character that I would be better off suppressing than encouraging with this gratuitously masochistic project. For a man who is as much a glutton for sex as I am, who indulges his senses and lives an intensely physical life, I am a strangely unearthly person, a latter-day stylite, a Christian

DIARY OF A DRAG QUEEN

ascetic, a would-be Capuchin monk in a mail-order cowl. Denial is both a whore and a hermit, a terrorist and a mystic.

It is a commonplace among my female friends that I am experiencing firsthand the truth of that tired old adage, "It is difficult to be a woman," but this is not quite accurate since I am actually discovering how *impossible* it is to be one and how huge a commitment of time and effort one must make, not only on the purchase of clothing and the application of makeup, but on such hygienic rituals as my dreaded weekly shaving sessions. Every Friday, I pluck my eyebrows and shave my upper thighs, all that is really necessary since I never remove my stockings during sex (although, to prevent myself from developing the furry calves of a centaur, I take a few cursory swipes with my razor once every other Friday). I loathe these weekly self-mutilations, not only because they complicate the minimal beauty regimen I was accustomed to performing as a man but also because my inner thighs erupt in protest into fields of infected blemishes, disfiguring my only good feature with splotches that, unless I take the added precaution of concealing them with the opaque "crèmes" in my "post-op correction kit" (intended to cover the scars left by major surgery), appear distinctly contagious and venereal. I have done extensive research on preventing these flare-ups and have slowly learned to control the worst of them with frequent applications of cortisone cream and a medicated powder but I am always on the lookout for new ways of simplifying the process, techniques that, as a rule, only make matters worse, the pimples pussier, the pores more inflamed, leaving me with the tantalizing complexion of a recently plucked chicken.

I have experimented with waxing and depilatories like Nair, both of which have turned my legs into mottled, leprous eyesores. Nair, I've discovered, actually causes scabbing on my inner thighs and when I first used it on my chest, slathering my breasts and belly with this viscid goop, I cauterized my nipples, which began to bleed, a reaction made all the more disturbing by the foul smell of the substance, a miasmal stench made even more repulsive by the sickly-sweet fragrances the company uses to mask the vile odor of a battery acid that sloughs off, not only thousands of hair follicles, but an ounce or two of flesh as well.

My maiden voyage waxing my legs was also a catastrophe. The tub of resin I purchased from my local beauty supply store came without directions, and so I simply followed the example of my friend Amelia, who one night demonstrated to me how she waxed her chin by expertly twirling a dollop of bluish taffy with a pair of chopsticks and then slapping the mess on her face where it solidified into a gray cap. The whole procedure looked so effortless that I confidently smeared a swath of melted resin from my knee to my hip and then waited for it to harden. And waited and waited. I applied water to cool it, I massaged it with ice, I dabbed it with paper towels, but no matter how much time elapsed, it remained as sticky as orange marmalade and, what's more, began oozing in rivulets down the sides of my thigh until I felt as doomed in my bedaubed state as a seagull in an oil spill. Everywhere I turned, my desperate flappings left gummy patches of resin, now on my doorknobs from my tacky fingers, now on the back of my desk chair, which collided accidentally with my thigh. I tried every detergent I could find—soap, mineral oil, cleansers for scouring the sink, and then, finally, as my panic approached hysteria and I began to imagine my entire apartment covered with a thin film of glue, paint thinner, which I applied while sitting in the tub, rubbing myself clean with the abrasive pad I use to clean my pots. Needless to say, the following day, my thighs were raw bratwursts which, when I met a trick that evening, I simply stuffed in a pair of hose like sausages in fishnets.

And so I have experienced one of the countless behind-the-scenes tragedies that torment the would-be odalisque, who lives the double life of a kind of high-fashion secret agent, perpetually passing off the arduous and not infrequently quite painful efforts

DIARY OF A DRAG QUEEN

that go into her public presentation as unburdensome procedures that she is capable of performing with her hands tied behind her back, the implication being that she is gorgeous and smooth as a baby's bottom quite naturally, that she wakes up in the morning as fresh and dewy as Aphrodite. Sadly, I myself wake up as hairy, hungover, and ill-tempered as Cerberus, and the evidence of the blood, sweat, and tears that go into my drag regimen are painfully obvious in the strata of cosmetic layers that all too visibly cake my cheeks and sink into the furrows of my forehead.

Him

How does one address an odalisque, even one so clearly exhausted by the effortlessness of her beauty? According to the men who contact me online, as "baby," "honey," "hun," "darling," "sweetheart," "sweetie," "love," "luv," "lovie," "dear," "dearie," and "baby doll." When men cruise the Internet, they resort to a saccharine and highly infantilized idiom of feminine endearments. Anyone who has been even remotely affected by the feminist movement will recoil from the amorous pet names with which those on the prowl patronize their prey. The word "woman" may have replaced the faintly derogatory "girl" in common parlance but, in chivalrous online chatter, one is never a woman but a "lady," a word that is, appearances notwithstanding, actually a linguistic concession to women's lib. Men have responded to the new climate of political sensitivity, not by using "woman," a word they find too clinical, insufficiently expressive of their adoration, but by resorting to a label whose fulsomeness they believe radiates respect, "lady" connoting both deference and old-fashioned, lovelorn sentimentality. Such is the outcome of decades of bickering about forms of address, a battle that women never really won since men felt that they overcame their chauvinism by turning on the courtly charm and wooing "ladies" with faintly antiquated forms of coquetry.

Men out hunting transsexuals and transvestites also use the word "lady" because they are, after all, flattering men, people who have grounds to feel uncertain about their gender and who therefore appreciate their suitors' constant assurances that they are feminine enough to do honor to the name. In this sense, the word "lady" is not as ideologically jarring to them as it is to me since I do not have as much invested in the disguise as pre-ops or transsexuals do.

Her

O r is this true? I have to admit that I secretly like being called "lady" and "baby" and "hun." I like masculine men wooing me, flirting with me, chasing me around the table like a lecherous boss chasing his secretary, partly because, before AIDS, gay men fucked rather than flirted. At last, I am being treated like a princess, spoiled with compliments, swept off my feet (or at least off my desk chair) by these online Romeos. It is a novel experience to participate in the old song-and-dance between the sexes, the chase, the gallant pursuit, a type of lovemaking that is entirely foreign to me, not only because I am gay and approach sex with the average male's predatory sexual instincts, but because even among gay men I am somewhat frigid and unapproachable. I have never had the time to flirt, to squander hours that I would rather spend reading and writing, and so all of this billing and cooing has turned my head, flattering my vanity, the honeyed words soothing an ego always in need of being salved with compliments, especially now that I have undertaken a project that makes me so absurdly self-conscious.

Which leads me back to my old lament about menopause. I enjoy the fatuous things these men call me because I know that a time will come, sooner rather than later, when I will be lucky to be the object of such gallantry. As a middle-aged gay man, I have naturally lost my sexual edge, even if drag has temporarily rewarded me with a reprieve from my long, slow decline into the sexlessness of old age. I regret the ultimate loss of my familiar pastime of cruising not only on the narcissistic grounds that I will be less admired, my ego unstroked, but on the social grounds that I will be deprived of my chief weapon for warding off the loneliness of the study. I am so desperate about becoming celibate because the whore's voracity has made the recluse's seclusion, not pleasant certainly, but at least endurable. Tricking is not primarily about indulging my senses but about achieving human contact in a life devoid of social opportunities. For thirty years, my body and its attractiveness have been my bridge with the mainland, my sole defense against absolute solitude, and now that I have grown old, I will be forced to retire into deeper and deeper seclusion. When Denial is finally packed away, I will have hung up not only her teddies but the wiles that my whorish sister employed in order to keep the recluse in some kind of contact, however superficial, with the rest of humanity. The hermit and the whore are the closest of friends, and when the whore severs this intimate relationship and withdraws from the playing field, the hermit will have lost his caretaker, the forbearing nurse who ministered to his social needs, who pushed him around the grounds of his hermitage.

Him

My lovers are better at flirting than fucking. While I have maintained a slam-bam attitude toward sex all of my life, cruising parks and bathhouses, my online suitors have been forced to live in their imaginations, since women seldom put out without a long assault, a love siege that men hope will starve them into submission. Hence, while I am likely to interpret men's flattery, their mash notes and lovelorn valentines, their e-mails-doux, as invitations to sex, they view their carryings-on as sexual acts in and of themselves, an erotic pastime that they have learned rarely culminates in a kiss, let alone a fuck. The result is that, after whispering sweet electronic nothings in my ear and engaging in lengthy foreplay in the back seats of their cyber-mobiles, men almost never have the courage to meet, having spent their wad serenading me, and are alarmed when their prey takes them at their word, whips up her dress, and shamelessly offers them her charms on the spot. I come to sex as a man who wants immediate results and, what's more, has gotten immediate results for decades, whereas they come to sex as men for whom immediate results are little more than masturbatory fantasies, the stuff of daydreams, figments of that great incubator of performance anxiety, the imagination.

Under the circumstances, it isn't surprising that they rarely show up for the dates they make, or do so only 25–50 percent of the time, a low rate of return that infuriates me not only because I am sexually frustrated by constant no-shows but because their irresponsibility violates my schoolmarmish insistence on being polite to strangers. Do they feel any guilt at all about not contacting me to tell me they aren't coming? Is an online stranger just a cipher on the screen for them, an e-mail address, a disembodied P.O. box? Granted, performance anxiety is coupled with their fears of facing an unfamiliar situation, but I always give them painless ways of backing out without admitting their cowardice, asking them to either call or e-mail, a small courtesy that they seldom extend to me.

I have never felt more male than as a woman, never realized how much I moved like a man until I squatted in tight pantyhose in front of my refrigerator, how square my jaw was until I tried desperately to soften it with cosmetics, how ungainly my body until I minced down my hallway in spike heels, my hands slapping the walls for support. And yet in one regard, I find myself identifying so strongly with women that, for all intents and purposes, I *am* female: namely, in my impatience with men, with their irresponsibility, lack of consideration, preoccupation with their own interests to the exclusion of those of other people, and etc. and etc., the whole litany of clichés which seems highly original and pertinent now that I am the one wearing the fuck-me pumps. I did not feel this same degree of alienation from my gender when I was a man, not because I truly behaved like one, and not because gay men treat each other any better than straight men do, but simply because gay men routinely have anonymous sexual encounters and are therefore more likely to keep the dates they make, whereas straight men are all fantasy and no action. Rather than admitting their cowardice, they will inconvenience a stranger and feel absolutely no remorse, leaving me cursing like a jilted bride. It is not as if I want them to be more attentive, more attuned to "my feelings," more generous with their flattery, more open with their emotions, more demonstrative with their love. I do not want to be showered with presents or bouquets of roses or servile adoration. I want them to keep the dates they make with me, god-damn it all, a small price to pay for uncomplicated sex without all of the usual burdens that women impose on men. The truth is that men are not too male to meet, but too female, too romantic, too accustomed to the abstract rigmarole of courtship to risk something as concrete, as devoid of protestations of eternal love, as a quick, anonymous screw in the hay.

Which brings me to one of my pet peeves about the Internet, the black picture it paints of humanity, which, if its online behavior is any indication, fully deserves obliteration by whomever has his finger on the button that opens those silos in Nevada. I may sound a little governessy, but I have never seen such shocking rudeness and cruelty as I have since I began cruising the Internet and threw myself into the electronic melting pot where I have had to undergo a crash course in Darwinian ethics, in survival of the fittest, as well as in cryptography, since for the first time in my life I have encountered gross illiteracy. As an intellectual, one hears about this scourge from the distance, but it remains unimaginable, since all of one's friends and acquain-tances speak and write English well, unlike teenagers who, at their most eloquent, write prose that resembles the nonsensical strings of numbers, exclamation points, and ampersands that cartoonists use to represent expletives. The Internet has forced me to take a cold plunge into the icy waters of democracy, and I am sickened by what I see, at once appalled by the gratuitous brutality of scoundrels, however young, who exploit the cover of anonymity to give free rein to their sadism, and disheartened by the implications of mass illiteracy for my profession, which never seems so useless as when I am trapped in a chat room like a character in a bad play.

Her

It is better to remain indoors in a chat room, however, than to venture out into the streets. Only once, late one drunken December night, did I bundle myself up and go to a corner bodega for a beer run in my makeup, wig, and heels, but I have never repeated this foolhardy excursion. In fact, I dread stepping out of my apartment in my getups as much as vampires dread stepping out into sunlight. I live in terror that my neighbors should discover what I am doing, that I should forget that I am made up (a surprisingly simple oversight) and come to the door to take a package they have accepted for me, or, horror of horrors, that I should be caught in the hallway or the elevator when, after the outside doors to the buzzers lock at 10:00 P.M., I am forced to go down to meet a trick in one of my clownish disguises. For these fantastic voyages, I wear sunglasses and hooded sweatshirts pulled tightly over my face, the costumes of a hysterical actress bent on avoiding the attention of her intrusive fans, but only attracting more of it by virtue of her ostentatious stealth. The building's 10:00 curfew, imposed when the neighborhood was at the mercy of drug pushers and crack addicts, instills me with dread on those nights that I go on a drag bender, drunk and horny. To leave my apartment is to enter a war zone of unexpected encounters, ambushes by astonished families returning late from Grandma's or packs of black teenage boys who smoke pot in the stairwells. I tell my tricks to hurry, to get here before 10:00, to do everything they can to arrive before the building's security timer turns the bolt and I am exposed to the elements, as if I were Cinderella forced to flee the ball in a coach that will soon become a pumpkin, my lovely raiments—rags.

I pride myself on my iconoclasm, savor the righteousness of the saintly outcast, the terrorist in a teddy, and yet do I really have the strength of my convictions? What kind of terrorist am I if I am so easily cowed by the prospect of being caught that I won't cross the threshold of my apartment unless I hide every trace of drag, lowering my face in shame for fear that someone should see how heavily made up it is? How carefully I transgress this sexual taboo, anxious lest I offend community standards, harrow the souls of God-fearing families in the elevator, expose myself to their ridicule! For a terrorist, I am remarkably timorous, in fact, insufferably polite. I explode my bombs, not in the street, but in my bedroom—cap guns and firecrackers which I muffle with pillows for the sake of men who clap like delighted schoolboys at the harmless detonations of my iniquitous games.

My tricks do not understand the suspense of the perpetually looming curfew because they assume that I am a full-time "woman" and therefore that I would have no qualms about meeting them in public, let alone at the door to my building. It is important to them to think that I live in drag, and I have often deceived them on the subject, implying that I go to work in sensible heels, a conservative pleated skirt, and a white blouse with a floppy bow and that I walk around my apartment wearing my wigs and panties. It is vital to their belief in my femininity that they think of me as a transvestite rather than as an occasional cross-dresser, an illusion that aids their willing suspension of disbelief. Somehow, through the tortuous logic of those eager to be deceived, they can find my femaleness plausible if I tell them that I never break out of character, that I have erased my gender, that the disguise is not detachable, a mask that can be donned and doffed at my convenience. They must be convinced that I am not fooling them but fooling myself instead, that they are not the dupes of a masquerade but its stage managers, that they are humoring a fetishist, participating in the fantasy of a nutcase who thinks he's Napoleon. To enjoy their fetish of having sex with men in women's clothing without guilt, they must cast the onus of their perversion on my shoulders. For me to enjoy *my* fetish of having sex with heterosexual men who have sex with gay men, I must in turn cast the onus of my perversion onto theirs, believing that what they really want is a woman, not a male, that they desire, not me, but someone else. One fetish does indeed scratch the other fetish's back.

No matter what I tell my suitors, I cannot "pass." When I was still a gay man, I was able to maintain the fiction of my masculinity, so essential to my sexual success, only by remaining inert and silent, for the second I began to speak, the cat leapt out of the bag and I laughed and gesticulated in ways that other homosexuals find unattractive, although they themselves—unconsciously, it goes without saying—constantly let down their hair and giggle like schoolgirls, all the while convinced, belligerently so, that they are gruff, stolid, and masculine. But just when I have freed myself from the threat of effeminacy, which is now a real advantage, I find that my sexual viability is jeopardized by the very opposite threat, that of masculinity, which emerges in my deep, sonorous voice, as feminine as night is day. I have lost many, many tricks by agreeing to talk to them on the telephone before we meet. During these mortifying if mercifully short conversations, I try to modulate my voice into a husky Dietrich whisper, a breathy falsetto that I cannot sustain and that, like the squawk of an adolescent boy, frequently sheds an octave by accident, plummeting from B-flat to C-sharp. As I make love to the receiver, purring into their ears, making my tongue lazy and stupid, babbling girlishly about what I am wearing or what I like to do in bed, always with a slight hesitation, as if I were ashamed to be so candid, so unladylike, I am honestly surprised that they don't laugh at me outright or hang up the phone, convinced that I am playing a practical joke on them. Instead, they respond to me as if there were nothing whatsoever unnatural about someone saying in a voice far deeper than their own that he is presently wearing nothing but fishnet stockings and a thong and that he finds a pair of sheer pantyhose the perfect attire for lounging about the house. In fact, a number of men *have* hung up the phone and many have commented that my voice isn't feminine enough for them, although just as many seem to have appreciated the spirit of the performance, if not its success, and told me that they loved my "little voice," a somewhat flabbergasting fib and one that suggests how willingly horny men, God bless their filthy compulsions, suspend disbelief, indeed cast it to the winds.

My attempts to overcome the limitations of my inept mimicry of girlishness extend as far as my answering machine, which now announces "I am not at home to take your call" in an inaudible murmur so ethereal that my friends regularly complain that there is something wrong with my tape, that they can barely hear me— as indeed is my intention since I have, I must confess, been too liberal with my phone number, essentially writing it on the walls of every toilet in cyberspace. When people call, I now have to pause before I reach for the receiver, weighing in my mind the likelihood of its being a friend or a trick, someone who expects to hear a man's voice or a woman's. It is embarrassing to say "hello" in my normal sepulchral tone of voice only to switch abruptly to my lisping purr when a startled male from a chat room calls me, although it is much worse when I affect a sultry Eartha Kitt growl only to hear a good friend ask doubtfully, "Daniel?" In such cases, my heart skips a beat and I awkwardly revert to the pretentious patrician accent that my friends know so well.

The shortcomings of my voice were brought home to me yesterday when an Adonis I met online told me that he would love to meet me but that I would have to do him a favor before he would have sex with me: allow him to tie me up and tickle me. I have never allowed any man to tie me up nor, for that matter, to tickle me, but I was sorely tempted in his case because of his beauty and so I asked him if he would be willing to forgo the ropes, which, for the pleasure of jabbing me in the ribs and torturing the soles of my feet, he claimed he was. I was just about to e-mail him my address and phone number when it suddenly occurred to me that there was one major problem: If he wanted to reduce me to helpless peals of laughter, I would indeed—there was no way around it—have to laugh. Sure, I can ham it up with my Marlene Dietrich routine, but the prospect of having to titter madly, squealing like a stuck pig, my hands fluttering in a blur to bat him away, was simply too preposterous, and I had to refuse him, lest we end up really and truly laughing—at me—hyperventilating at my lame efforts to sound feminine.

Him

From time to time as I write this diary, I will perform a taxonomy of fetishists as my understanding of the complex psychology of this attraction develops. Already, I have had to revise my thinking, for I now recognize that there isn't a single type but many types, all of whom find something quite different in drag queens and transsexuals.

The simplest to understand is the Horny Straight Male. He is an opportunist who is willing to overlook the imperfections of the disguise for the sake of a good blow job, which he has heard through the sexual grapevine, correctly as everyone knows, is more expertly administered by men than by women. He is not interested in drag as a phenomenon in itself but only as a costume that conceals the gender of his fellator, whom he rarely fucks, let alone touches. If he has any greater interest in the encounter, it lies in the pressure men feel to "experiment," a word that essentially disguises his need to put another notch in his bedpost as liberal openness—even unconventionality—although there seems to me nothing whatsoever unconventional about kicking back for a blow job, unless of course unconventionality is taken to mean infrequency, in which case the act is highly unconventional since women are seldom willing to submit without reciprocation to such a selfish and one-sided type of sex.

Horny straight males are among my favorite conquests. For

one, the fact that they would settle for a sluttish Madame Tussaud mannequin who lurks in the shadows, allowing herself to be seen only under light of the lowest wattage, suggests that they are very horny indeed. For another, as a gay man who, on the level of his libido if not on the level of his political consciousness, sincerely believes that straight men are more authentically male than gay ones, horny heterosexuals have always been the holy grail of my fantasy life and the first and foremost reason that I am performing this charade. I am not one to believe that I must behave in a wholesome fashion and suppress desires that are clearly self-loathing. What's more, I will not excuse myself by saying that my masquerade, far from representing, as it unquestionably does, a degrading concession to politically retrograde fantasies, is an attempt to purge these demeaning ideas "out of my system." I *will* say, however, that, whatever my motive, in the act of fulfilling this heterosexual fantasy of mine, I am actually destroying it. Familiarity breeds contempt and, having now had sex with quite a few of my fantasy men, the mystery caused by their inaccessibility has significantly diminished. Perhaps I will have learned, when I finally retire Denial and all of her outfits to the dark walk-in closet of my mind where she came from, what I have always known intellectually, that a cock is just a cock, a man a man, that they taste the same, smell the same, have the same bristly chins and hairy butts, regardless of their sexual preferences.

A second type of fetishist is the man who is actually a homosexual and whose interest in transvestites is exclusively genital. The drag aesthetic is beside the point for him, because dresses and wigs simply block out everything that is too compromisingly male, crop it from the picture, and allow him to focus his attention on a few square inches, which might just as well exist apart from the rest of his lover's anatomy. Eunuchs are said to preserve their lost manhood like keepsakes in precious boxes, and if this second type of fetishist were to have his way, I would simply lend him my box and saunter off down the hallway to resume my reading in

another room. Sex for him is an act of censorship, of willed ignorance, much as people in movie theaters close their eyes during the
scary parts and then open them when the coast is clear, seeing only
what they want to see. No drag queen wants to be treated like the
contents of a eunuch's box. She wants to be loved for more than
her genitals but for her labor, for the success of her impersonation,
for her virtuoso performance, the arduous ordeal involved in over-
coming the obstacles of her gender. Sex with the repressed homosexual is, in my experience, almost always disastrous, far more so
than with the horny heterosexual, who is entirely indifferent to my
body but whose unresponsiveness confirms my belief in his
authenticity, for how could he really be straight if he evinced
curiosity about the "surprise," the "something a little extra," as
drag aficionados call it, hiding beneath the Lycra teddy? Sadly, I
attract quite a few of the eunuch's-box type of fetishist, mainly
because, in their eagerness to fondle the "surprise," my dowdy
appearance is of little importance to them, the only thing that matters being my cock and the slight concession I make—however
perfunctory—to femininity.

Third, there are those who like both the sluttish look *and* the
cock. They are the genuine fetishists, the ones who actively seek
out transvestites and may even prefer them to women. They are
not looking for a girl or for a boy, but for an androgyne, for a
chimera that occupies an anatomical limbo between the sexes, a
self-created hermaphrodite who combines "the best of both
worlds," as my tricks often justify their preferences when I question them. These men are bisexual and are also the best and most
appreciative lovers, given that they admire the whole drag gestalt
and do not view the transvestite as just a convenient sperm recep-
tacle or a eunuch's box.

For much of my life, I have thought of masculinity and femininity as two contradictory aesthetics. The sexual attraction to
both, despite popular gay-lib legends, rarely coexists in the same
mind, and yet here in the androgyne lover these aesthetics lie

cheek-by-jowl in all of their glaring irreconcilability. And yet perhaps the secret to the appeal of this new aesthetic is that the conflict between these divergent forces is never fully resolved, creating a new dissonant aesthetic based on a seductive alliance of contradictions. When men look at a drag queen, they experience a disturbing sense of paradox that is easily eroticized. On the one hand, they feel an instantaneous attraction to someone feminine; on the other, they recoil from someone clearly masculine. The result is a volatile mixture of discordant responses to incongruities that can create emotions more intense than mere physical attraction alone, the element of repulsion heightening desire much as the taste of something salty heightens the taste of something sweet. That which repels is found in the same body as that which attracts, and the feeling of irresolution and conflict acts as a powerful aphrodisiac. Some would look at the bisexual transvestite lover as proof that sexual categories are fluid, but perhaps rather than giving the lie to these categories, his behavior confirms their unambiguous opposition.

There is at least a fourth category of transvestite lover whose fascination with drag I don't fully understand: the fellow (or sister) cross-dresser, the man who wants to have sex with another tv, almost always as the dominant partner, like the hirsute Sicilian from Staten Island who admitted to me that he made "a damn awful drag queen," a confession born out by his photograph, that of a dour prison matron, a lesbian sadist at a state correctional facility, with furry forearms and unshaven legs. Months ago, I met online an athlete from Queens, a truly beautiful man with a gorgeous body and all-American good looks, who sent me a photograph of himself provocatively lifting the hem of a shapeless Pollyanna dress, no doubt a flea-market find, a somewhat macabre image especially since he was wearing no makeup other than an obscene gash of glistening red lipstick. He professed to be straight but he also claimed to enjoy doing drag and fucking other tvs or to have sex *after* the tv forces him to engage in a game of dress-up, an act of humiliation that is perhaps his real interest in cross-dressing and one that women may simply be unwilling to perform. I told him that I wasn't interested, that I would only make love with him as a man, but he pleaded with me, finally begging me to make a single concession and allow him, pretty please, to wear one symbolic feminine item, say, a pair of thigh-highs, a request that seemed so pathetic that it would have been petty of me not to grant it, especially in light of his good looks (I did, however—perhaps cruelly—exact a concession from him in turn, that he wear a jock-strap, a favor with which he was, it goes without saying, hesitant to comply).

We never met and I have remained mystified by this extremely common type of cross-dresser ever since. Perhaps he wants to act out a lesbian scene, fantasizing that he is a diesel dyke thrusting his womanhood on his compliant femme, and again perhaps he settles for another cross-dresser because most women refuse to participate in such kinky sex and view transvestism as I do, as the ultimate forfeiture of masculinity. It is possible, however, that straight cross-dressing is not a forfeiture at all but a homage to femininity, an instance of radical heterosexuality by men so in love with women that they want to feel what they feel, slip into their skin, don their clothing, know the pleasure of straight sex from the point of view of their mates. Why they would do this with a cross-dresser rather than a woman doesn't seem to fit the theory, unless of course it is an act of desperation caused by the scarcity of cooperative girls or maybe even by the humiliation of travestying their manhood in front of an audience that wants them to prove it, to flaunt it, factors that might very well lead them to seek out men in the same boat.

Peter belongs to my third category, that of the man who genuinely loves the drag-queen look, although like most men he prefers transsexuals to cross-dressers. When I met him online months ago, he generously volunteered to give me a show on his webcam, and for some fifteen minutes or even longer, I sat with my nose glued to the screen as he said and did indelicate things that no respectable gentleman should ever say or do to a lady. He performed a sort of cyber lap dance, while I sat in my desk chair, a voyeur peeping through the keyhole of the Internet, which had magically opened up a gray, grainy vista onto an unmade bed in a room in Queens. After a few minutes, as he continued his demonstration with no end in sight, he admitted to me that he refused to have an orgasm, not because he couldn't or didn't want to, but because it was Lent and he, a good Catholic boy from Bensonhurst, had chosen to refrain from orgasm as his penance— although—such are the miraculous contradictions of religion—atonement for his sins did not preclude jerking off before horny drag queens salivating over his naked body on the Web. For several days, I played Mephistopheles and tempted him to abandon his resolution, asking for longer, hotter sessions, becoming more and more shameless with the dirty talk that I pounded out on the keyboard to encourage his exhibitionism, begging him to cum, implying that the fate of his eternal soul could not possibly hang on something as inconsequential as an orgasm. But no matter what irreligious snares I set up to lure him from the path of righteousness, he made his mother proud and remained true to his beliefs.

We finally met in person and he was every bit as delicious as his webcam had promised. Better still, he was smart and considerate. After sex, we spoke of his involvement with transsexuals and the return from Malaysia or Singapore of his recently gelded girlfriend, now at home swaddled in bandages. It was from him that I learned some of the hard facts of the scene, that the hormones the pre-ops take cause extreme emotional volatility and that the rate of suicide among those who actually submit to the knife is staggeringly high, not surprising since, once they have cut themselves free from the burden of the "surprise," the "something a little extra," they become just ordinary girls in men's eyes and seldom even very pretty girls at that. Peter was a sweet and intelligent man, and there was something almost tragic that this gentle soul should be condemned to emotional turmoil in his love life because his preferred partners existed in a state of physical as well as psychological upheaval. He spoke patiently about their torments, but it was clear that their instability exasperated him even as he reaped the erotic benefits of their drug-induced psychosis.

Her

The drugs also make them a menace to poor Denial. Yesterday afternoon, I again suffered a brutal series of attacks by my chat-room detractors, who by now draw everyone's attention to my extreme ugliness every time I enter the room, repeating ad nauseam their joke that I am "very heavy metal," Ozzy Ozbourne, Gene Simmons from the band KISS, and advising me to go kill myself, to put myself out of my misery once and for all by jumping off the Brooklyn Bridge or slashing "yur rists." Try as I might, I cannot take this sophomoric ridicule in stride and, in addition to feeling the humiliation of being homely enough to sour milk, feel the humiliation of allowing myself to be humiliated by such small fry, by uneducated teenage boys who have turned the Internet into a bully's playground where they gain prestige among their peers by deriding the "nerds" and "retards." I think with despair that this is what I've come to: At the age of forty-six, after a lifetime of study, after three books and countless essays, I squander my days providing rowdy young boys with a bull's-eye for target practice, setting myself up as the honored victim of their potty mouths, the deeply chagrined recipient of their spitballs and paper airplanes. I have mentioned before that Denial is not me but a prosthesis, but it is as if my wooden leg is acquiring sensation, experiencing shooting pains that radiate all the way down from the silicone socket to the rubberized foot.

Just after my online mauling, I went to the grocery store where I witnessed one of the managers trying to shoo away a decrepit black drag queen, obviously homeless, who had parked herself at the entrance begging for change. She remained quite adamant that she wouldn't budge and the manager was forced to storm back inside, defeated by this battered wreck of a human being who wore a blanket pinned around her waist for a dress and had three protruding rotten teeth and a hank of molting Afro jutting out of an otherwise-bald head. When I left the store, I handed her all of my change and she flashed me a jack-o'-lantern smile, immediately recognizing that I was gay. "How very kind of you!" she exclaimed, putting on the unlikely airs of an Upper East Side matron, and then, giving me the once-over, dropped her airs and added, "And you have a nice little body there, nice ass, very well put together." After the rounds I had spent sparring on the bully's playground, I experienced a moment of genuine solidarity with this pariah and was overwhelmed with that proverbial feeling of "There but for the grace of God go I," even though I realize that it is virtually impossible that I should plunge so low unless I should become addicted to crack, as she obviously was. Having just served as the chat room's papier-mâché piñata, I felt that there was something almost prophetic about the coincidence of meeting a creature who might as well represent a twin destiny, as vilified on the sidewalks as I was on the computer screen.

But am I really the victim I make myself out to be? The ostracized are capable of feeling the moral certainty of the martyr who revels in a virtuousness bestowed upon her by her unjust treatment. When I was nine years old and wore my big boots to elementary school, was I not taunting the mob into banishing me, and was I not seeking in the injustice of this act proof of my moral superiority? In drag I enter the quasi-holy state of the saintly outcast who acquires in virtue what she loses in social approval. Drag for me is thus not only a way of regaining my youth in the face of the ravages of menopause, but of tempting the crowd into wronging me, into exhibiting its narrow-minded puritanism, making me suffer for my crimes against nature and in the process allowing me to gain spiritual ascendancy over my oppressors. Ever since I put on my ugly shoes, I have used ostracism to set myself above my peers in the privileged ranks of the aggrieved, and drag is just the latest incarnation of this ancient psychological impulse, this tendency to hand my society a whip and then eagerly bare my shoulders for a salutary flogging. St. Lucy carries her eyes on a platter and St. Agatha proffers her breasts; St. Denial presents to the viewer unique attributes, the falsies and fake lashes of her own martyrdom.

Vengeance for both me and the black drag queen came the following evening when I entered the NYCShemale4male chat room to submit to yet another stoning, only to find that my nemesis, the chief heckler of the pack, was himself being stoned for his constant rudeness and compulsive denigration of the appearance and profession (prostitution) of the regular girls. I am not sorry that I picked up the biggest rock I could find and hurled it at his screen, joining in the fray with bloodthirsty glee, screaming for his immediate court-martial and summary execution. It was perfectly thrilling to watch him cowering there, pelted by a shower of insults, outnumbered, outgunned, even whining at one point that it wasn't fair that everyone should pick on him at once and that, if we wanted to fight, we should each take our turn. I feel somewhat vindicated by his downfall, however temporary, even as I realize that the chat room lynched him in the same spirit that they lynched me and that his crucifixion by no means suggests that the online mob has acquired a sense of fairness and remorse, just that anyone, provided they are sentient enough to feel and express pain, can serve as a sacrificial victim for a crowd that solidifies its identity as a group, its esprit de corps, through its collective killing sprees.

Last night my new elbow-length gloves snagged on my earrings. No sooner did I manage to get the studs through my relatively recent, perpetually infected piercings than my red Lycra fingertips would stick to the rhinestones and rip them back out again until I felt like a cat chasing a mouse on a string, pouncing on my prey at the very moment it was yanked away from me. It is difficult for us all to accept the fact that we are just another object in a world of objects, but it is even harder for a woman, since everything she wears, every bracelet, bobby pin, barrette, eye hook, zipper, snap, strap, strip of fringe, cashmere sweater, crepe de chine dress, lace teddy, and chiffon slip, adheres to the myriad thorns, thistles, and spurs that lie waiting in ambush for her to pass. She is a walking Velcro strip. Perhaps nature sees her as a mode of public transportation, a crosstown bus for prickly seedlings and spores that need to move on to more fertile grounds and therefore delight in plucking at her dress, pulling her hair, laddering her stockings.

To be a woman is to experience human maladjustment to the constraints and inconvenience of the physical world in a manner that is far more intense than the way men experience them. Early on in my life in drag, the hazards of my newfound adhesiveness left many of my costumes in tatters, as when, at an indelicate moment, the cheap wire fittings of the $1.99 bracelet I was wearing got stuck in my fishnet stockings so that I was forced to complete the act with one arm pinned to my side, running lopsidedly to the bathroom as soon as we had consummated our love in order to liberate myself with one enraged rip. On several occasions, sex has been interrupted by necklaces inadvertently catching in wayward fingers and exploding into showers of beads, and once my five-inch-long Las Vegas showgirl earrings became entangled in my wig and then hooked into my lace gown so that when I turned my head, writhing in ecstasy, my hair turned with it, coming to rest at a position some 90° west of where it was intended to be worn. Everything snags and catches—everything, that is, except for the things we *want* to snag and catch, like the minute snaps on the crotches of leotards or the hooks of my bra, which I have taken to fastening before I put it on, stepping into it, and then wriggling it up over my hips, waist, and shoulders. Women are supposed to float through the world on a cloud of diaphanous lace, trailing fluttering silk scarves, their necklaces and earrings dangling, glittering, tinkling like bells. In fact, however, our evanescence, our immaterial presence, defies our powers as illusionists. The lighter we are, the heavier we fall. No sooner do we loft up into the ether than some goblin from the world of splinters and ragged edges snatches us by the stocking and jerks us back down, cackling over the hubris of our pretensions to weightlessness. The heels of our stilettos lodge in cracks and stubbornly remain behind as we march bravely forward into the void, falling facefirst on cobblestone sidewalks. Our earrings snare in the shoulders of the suit jackets of the men who embrace us. Our world is barbed wire, and we are the advancing infantry impaled on its rusty thorns.

Him

The other night I met a black man from Bushwick, a college-educated guy who had recently lost his job as an intern for a local politician. He came bearing party favors, a six-pack of beer and a "blunt" longer and fatter than any cigar I have ever seen in my life, but the mood of the evening was anything but celebratory, possibly because the specter of unemployment hovered over our encounter and may even have been its precipitating cause, anguish driving him into the arms of the most immediately available source of comfort. He was not, however, an easy man to console or, indeed, to like, for it was not only him that I was expected to befriend but his inseparable companion, the chip on his shoulder. He was seething with resentment, angered by the failure of the world to lend him the hand he felt he deserved, to recognize his intelligence, which he demonstrated to me by making frequent references to Artaud, Heidegger, and Foucault. He tossed off these allusions with a supercilious air of triumph, delighted to see me cowed into silence by his erudition, when, in fact, the cause of my speechlessness lay in my tongue which, stoned out of its taste buds, as I was out of my mind, cleaved to the roof of my mouth every time I opened it.

He was an object lesson in the wisdom of Pope's couplet: "A little learning is a dangerous thing; Drink deep, or taste not the Pierian spring." He had had enough schooling to cultivate a certain glib sophistication, but he mistook a very limited range of references to stereotypical "hard" books as a liberal-arts education in and of itself. I seldom allow others to flaunt their intelligence at my expense and so the patronizing air he adopted toward the dumb trannie sprawled in a marijuana stupor at his side irritated me profoundly. Worse, I was unable to defend myself since every time I attempted to lift my heavy head spinning in a vortex of anger and paranoia, I slurred my words, incomprehensible gibberish came gushing out of my mouth, and I slumped back onto the bed, my wig askew, quite literally unable to rise to the occasion. I abhor the passive role intellectually, as much as I adore it sexually.

Her

Perhaps this is an appropriate place to discuss further the role of my library in my recreational activities, a prop that is key to this comedy of manners, functioning almost as a third character in the plot of my sex life. My front door opens onto a room full of books arranged in tiered shelves that descend from the highest case, which stands just under eight feet, to the lowest, which stands just over two, forming an imposing staircase that I have upholstered with a bright red runner, now somewhat mossy from months—possibly as much as a year—of careless housework. My books immediately establish in strangers' minds my education and class and, what's more, they are the one aspect of my real life that I allow my tricks to see, the sole part of me that isn't in drag, the authentic self, which I am never able to abandon in its entirety, since to do so would be to forfeit a central claim to my visitors' respect. How tenaciously the old Daniel Harris clings to his established identity as a writer even in the middle of a costume party in which he hopes against all hope to be mistaken for someone else—but not so entirely mistaken that his admirers cannot recognize that he is a serious, educated person, that despite the fancifulness, the plain silliness, of his girlish disguise, he reads widely and ambitiously, that he went to graduate school and has published three books. In fact, I cannot even imagine what it would be like were I to meet my tricks on neutral ground, say, in a cinder-block room devoid of my possessions, a propless cell in which I would have no external way of identifying myself to my lovers as an intellectual but would have to confront them naked as a newborn babe, unencumbered by the baggage of my drawings and art books. I suspect I would find such a situation intolerable and would panic to lose everything that testifies to my social standing, panic because I have so little to cling to as it stands, because my identity as a writer is so tenuous that I cannot easily force the cantankerous intellectual elitist imprisoned within my outfits to take an impromptu holiday, like a maid given an afternoon off by a mistress who wants to misbehave. I also panic because the more of myself that I surrender to drag, the more I treasure what remains of my real life. My little game of dress-up is perhaps taking a greater toll on me psychologically than I care to admit, for now that I have cause to question my identity, now that my career is stalled and my social life in ruins, it is perhaps inopportune to be experimenting with alternative selves rather than recycling the old one, as threadbare as it is, mending the rips, darning the holes, preventing it from unraveling before my very eyes.

After sex, my tricks often stop on the way out to bow before my literary altar, much as people from another age might have genuflected before an icon or a crucifix. They genuflect, moreover, in the same spirit of superstitious dread, with the same fear of the unknown, the same irrational trepidation about a divinity that, like the Christian god, is no longer relevant to their lives but to whom they pay perfunctory homage, thereby hedging their bets. How often I have stood behind them as they crouch before my shelves reading the spines of my Penguin Classics, exclaiming what a marvelous thing this mysterious monolith is, praise that I accept with ladylike nonchalance, pretending that I am modestly apathetic to words that in fact fill me with pride, a reaction that demoralizes me later when I consider how desperate I am to accept flattery, regardless of its source, whether from a truck driver, a mailman, or a security guard. The other evening I had sex with a cell-phone salesman who, like so many others, refused to look me in the eye, either because I am too ugly or, given my towering stature, too unsettling a presence. Afterward, I found myself standing behind him while he knelt before my books and complimented me on my collection. It occurred to me that he was making love to my library in a way that he could not bring himself to make love to me and that his compliments were like those of a man who praises a beautiful, younger sister in the presence of an older, homelier one. Far from being offended by his admiration of my brainy sibling, however, I was delighted, ours being an intimate family. His remarks bounced off my books and back onto me, perhaps not their intended target but, given how integral my collection is to my sense of selfhood, their de facto target.

As a connoisseur of self-doubt, I find myself examining my behavior for trace elements of disingenuousness, telltale signs of my failure to accept the full implications of my actions. Take, for instance, the way I have begun speaking to women at cosmetic counters. It is no longer very difficult for me to tell them that I am shopping for myself and that my purchases are intended for drag, although they all persist in the fiction that I am what they call a "performer," i.e., a professional drag queen who lip-synchs torch songs in clubs, an excuse they use either to protect themselves from the unspeakable thought that I am a perverted sexual fetishist or to protect *me* by pretending that they haven't a clue what I'm really up to. This said, I have yet either to lie or to undeceive them and therefore feel that, although I haven't been totally frank, I haven't compromised my puritanical integrity, which mandates that I refrain from lying even in the middle of the biggest whopper I've ever told.

I do, however, narrate my makeup tribulations in a way that may subtly fudge the truth. I speak about my face more or less as if it were a hubcap or a manhole cover. I claim to be so incompetent with my lipsticks and blushes that I might as well be pushing over my skin one of those spray-painting machines that road workers roll over the pavement in order to stencil white arrows and lay down the yellow no-passing lines. I cultivate a brusque, no-nonsense, almost-masculine manner when I describe my failed efforts to beautify myself, referring to the swaths of silver highlighter that give my cheekbones their unsightly metallic glare as "racing stripes," my over-pancaked, overpowdered face as a "cadaverous kabuki mask," and my irritated legs as "the killing fields." In effect, I tell them that I take none of this too seriously, that I know that I am ugly as sin, that I will never look pretty, that I am, in fact, not a real fetishist at all, some poor clown who is convinced he can pass as a woman, but am playing this game with detached and highly amused self-consciousness. I cannot bear the idea that anyone would think that I *think* that I am pretty, and therefore ham up my ineptitude and hideousness, talking about putting on makeup in a highly mechanical way, as if I were a grease monkey tuning a car, whipping up the hood, yanking out spark plugs, and siphoning off the antifreeze. I resort to the circumlocutions of fake candor, thereby escaping the embarrassment of my activities even as I am apparently being honest to a fault, even boorishly outspoken.

Daniel and Denial are very similar in this respect. Both are compulsive self-deprecators. In my last book, *A Memoir of No One in Particular,* I discussed how I have always tried to win over those who would mock me by being the first to make the joke about my most notably ridiculous characteristic, my effeminacy:

It is as if I believed that by assuming their critical point of view and acknowledging my absurdity I will forestall their heckling. Only unwitting dupes can be ludicrous, never those who embrace their preposterousness and demonstrate that they are fully aware of sticking out like a sore thumb, a recognition that short-circuits ridicule, since the presumably witless stooge shows that he too is laughing, indeed, that he is the one making the joke at his own expense, not the home boy trying to impress his girlfriend by yelling at a fag on the streets. By constantly maligning myself, I do my critics' work for them and beat them to the punch line, thus depriving them of the satisfaction of being the comedian, the entertainer, since I myself have appropriated this privileged position. . . . As early as my late teens, self-deprecation became a kind of dare, a wager I made with myself, a game of chicken in which I sought to find out how much self-knowledge I could tolerate.

Denial flourishes in part because I have added her to this wager, incorporated her ungainliness into my lifelong experiment with candor. She is yet another cliff in my endlessly repeated game of chicken. In *A Memoir of No One in Particular,* I strove (and perhaps failed) to be as honest as it is humanly possible to be about myself, and now I can extend this self-lacerating honesty to a whole new person with a whole new set of inhibitions and hang-ups—wounds that I can probe with the insistent needle of self-analysis.

But there is a way in which my lies, however slightly they stray from the truth, run parallel to it. There is, for instance, my entire personality as a drag queen which is a hyped-up, vampish version of the real Daniel Harris, who, even as a man, does indeed fancy himself an aging, faintly decadent femme fatale. This is one of the reasons that my girlish treble causes me such anguish, because, try as I might, I cannot sound sophisticated when I am lisping. As I warble and trill, I seem less like a woman than a character from *The Muppets,* Kermit the Frog or Miss Piggy, cartoon animals with falsetto whines, a far cry, figuratively speaking, from the foppish aesthete who spent five years at Harvard and who employs both his real voice and his library to remind his tricks who he really is, never letting them—indeed, never letting himself—forget that he is a substantial personage and not just an endearing oddity. I long to command the respect of an intelligent Lady, a grande dame, but the imperfections of my disguise and my lack of practice permit me to aspire no higher than a flirty soubrette, a cheap gum-smacking floozy from a hard-boiled novel, a cardboard character whose femininity resides partly in her ridiculousness.

I have spoken of the difficulties involved in feminizing my voice but I have neglected the challenges of walking and gesturing like a woman, another handicap that compromises both Denial's and Daniel's dignity. As a man, I move in a way that, sadly but truly, I believe others find languorous and sensual, but as a woman I must mince and wobble, never certain if my ankles will give way under the strain of their high altitude, making me crumple to the floor like a giraffe gunned down by a poacher on a heartbreaking episode of *Wild Kingdom,* a magnificent galloping beast collapsing in slow motion into a perfumed heap of synthetic hair and costume jewelry. Perhaps men don't want physical self-assurance in women. Perhaps imbalance, precariousness, is the essence of femininity, which must seem gauche and helpless, like Asian women with bound feet, whose shuffling gait makes them useless, ornamental.

I do not enjoy playing the fool, a klutz on stilts, perpetually off-kilter. The disguise is never so complete that I relinquish my core self, the elegant patrician with the fake British accent, who has spent his life trying to impress others with his eloquence and powers of discernment. Denial, like Eve, was created from Daniel's rib. She is not an entirely new construction and must avoid many aspects of stereotyped femininity that Daniel refuses or is unable to accept. What I resent when I am with men is, in short, that I cannot be a man, that *they* have all of the dignity, all of the self-possession, the physical power, the muscular grace, while I am treated like a bauble, a plush animal, a fluffy scented scratching post for horny guys to hump. When I am in drag, I relive the entire history of the feminist movement, from the suffragettes to the bra burners. I will never make a convincing woman, because I object on principle to key elements of the role.

Minutes ago I returned from the grocery store almost breathless with rage. It was my bad luck to end up dragging in tow a parade of eight skanky teenage girls, who, as is the wont of black teenagers when they amass in groups larger than two, began taunting me about my ass and my "fag walk" and laughing hysterically, with the cruel stupid maniacal laughter of the young when they are swept up by the ecstasy of the mob. They were only five feet behind me and either didn't care if I heard them or hoped that I would, because they made no effort to whisper but discussed me more or less as if I were, not a human being, but a computer-generated hologram, a pixellated special effect that had inexplicably materialized on Myrtle Avenue expressly for their amusement. It was hot, I was tired, the groceries were heavy and, what's more, I have been taunted on the streets once too often and so I turned to them and in my most ferocious voice said, "Why don't you just shut the fuck up?" A spray of braying laughter like a shower of glass hit me in the face and I lost complete control of myself. I cornered one of the girls and separated her from the pack, screaming at her, "Is this fun?!! Is this what you do for fun? You like making fun of strangers on the street? Is this fun now?" She continued to laugh, but even the ten feet that separated her from the mother ship were sufficient to take the wind out of her sails. A look of fear appeared on her face and her laughter became quieter and more forced, as if she were consciously willing her ridicule out of her body, using her lungs like a bellows. I walked on ahead of the group again and cornered another vulnerable stray who had drifted a few feet ahead of the pack, giving her the same treatment, asking in my shrillest voice with my most demonic look if she was "still having fun? Do you think it's fun to laugh at strangers on the street?" whereupon she darted back to the mother ship for protection. Having drawn the attention of the entire neighborhood, many of whom were laughing outright at me, I walked home cursing under my breath like a madman, imagining what it would have been like if I had pulled out a pistol and fired it into the air or, better still, gunned them down on the street, one after the next, as they deserved. Out of such fantasies are terrorists made. They are the cloth from which Denial was cut.

For a terrorist in a teddy, I am remarkably thin-skinned both in the chat rooms and on the streets where I am frequently catcalled (once by a boy no more than five or six years old, who called out "faggot" as I walked past his stoop). Rather than rolling off my back, such insults get under my skin and fester. One would assume that terrorists would be of sturdier mettle, but it would appear that, while I am courageous enough to desecrate sacrosanct categories of male and female, at heart I am a pussycat. Perhaps all terrorists are really pussycats. After all, they are by definition socially maladjusted, and maladjustment presupposes that some element of their society offended them so intensely that they refused to adapt, to conform to its strictures. Stolid, unemotional people are not easily offended and therefore do not feel compelled to hurl bombs, whereas the weak, the timid, the ineffectual are tormented by their society's barbarism and feel a strong incentive to take up weapons against it. There is a close connection between my courage and my cowardice; were I fearless, I would find nothing inordinately disturbing and would therefore have little to rebel against. Similarly, were I a complete coward, I would simply lie down and take it. My response to fear would be inaction. The recipe for the perfect terrorist is a mixture of both: sensitivity on the one hand, guts on the other.

Him

I am a terrorist with a conscience. Often during my adventures, I am haunted by a basic axiom of evolutionary science: that men with low status have less access to women. Their position at the bottom of the food chain compromises their sexual success, making them unattractive mates and, moreover, powerless in the face of the rivalry of men with greater resources, more allies, better guns, bigger bank accounts. A high percentage of the black men I meet (and living in Brooklyn I meet many) come to me out of desperation, because the typical homeboy or the "scrub," i.e., an unemployed black man living with his mother, cannot buy the charms of women who view sex in shockingly materialistic terms, as a bargaining ploy, a way of getting those diamond "rocks" that rappers in music videos are constantly draping around the necks of their typically café-au-lait girlfriends, who wriggle to the throb of their pitch-black boyfriends' music, surrounded by the princely trappings of nouveau riche opulence. In drag, I am the unsightly symbol of the exclusion of poor men from the mating game, of their slim chances of finding girls, at least the appetizing hip-hop ideal of the booty-shaking babe, whose scarcity they overcome by using a dolled-up surrogate, an effigy of racial injustice, the sop they are thrown in the face of their undeserved deprivation.

God knows I try to be a good sop, and god knows many if not most of my outcasts treat their effigy well, flatter her, pretend that she is beautiful, tell her gallant lies. Yesterday I met yet another poor black man. I was the third effigy that this nineteen-year-old had had sex with, the twelfth among all of his lovers, a number that put him at a distinct disadvantage in regard to experience, he being at least the 2,000th of mine. He was handsome, svelte, hung like a horse, and, for his age, a gifted sodomite, a kind of pederastic wunderkind. What's more, he, unlike most of the black men I meet, was in college getting his B.A. in accounting, a degree he fully intended to finish even though he had dreams of being the next Michael Jordan, spotted on the courts by a scout for the NBA and magically spirited away to a thirty-room mansion in Barbados, liberated from his grim fate as the son of a part-time house cleaner.

After sex, we sat side by side on the edge of the bed as I listened to him spell out his life plan, a remarkably sensible one that I praised for its farsightedness, hoping that my compliments would reinforce his resolve and contribute something, however small, to his ultimate success. On these occasions, I feel—indeed, I know—that I am acting as a privileged white cheerleader, rooting my lover on to victory, and I wonder if he finds my motivational rah-rahing patronizing or if he appreciates it for what it is, recognizes my genuine regret about the difficult odds he faces. I am too aware of feeling like a great white savior, a Lady Lincoln who has just been banged on her porch wearing a big hoopskirt by her manumitted Mandingo to feel comfortable with my role, but in the course of my adventures I constantly find myself stroking the egos—among other things—of black men, partly I suppose because I want to be admired as an abolitionist, a righteous crusader for equality. But perhaps because the intimacy of sex makes me sentimental, I feel sincere in my concern, as if my own anxiety to demonstrate my lack of prejudices, my limitless tolerance, were beside the point and what really mattered was that I leave my men with a kind of door prize: the gift of my affection, confidence, and esteem. It is as if the entire conflict between the races had briefly taken up residence in my bedroom and I could solve it right there on the spot with—such are the fantasies of good liberals—a kiss and a couple of compliments.

But not, of course, with cash, not, above all else, with the indignity of those insulting five-dollar bills.

Her

L ast night Amelia noticed that my false eyelashes were on backward, the right lash on the left eye, the left on the right. It would never even have occurred to me that the two are not interchangeable and I would have looked slightly cockeyed for my entire inglorious career as a drag queen had she not pointed out to me the simple fact that the shortest hairs must be glued nearest the nose. Amelia's consistently excellent advice has convinced her that Denial is *her* child, that she rescued her from the nightmare of her puberty, initiated her into the mysteries of cosmetics, escorted her on her maiden voyage, a sort of Virgil of the vagina. Although this is far from the truth, most of my information having been culled from the Internet and from picking the brains of the "artists" behind the makeup counters at Macy's and Sephora, she has certainly played an essential role in taking me, like Lulu in *To Sir With Love,* from crayons to perfume. In spite of being a lesbian *and* a top, indeed, *because* she is a lesbian and a top, she understands femininity as no one I have ever known and appreciates it both from the standpoint of an ardent admirer of women and an admirably sexy woman in her own right. For Amelia, the feminine is both an aesthetic and a science, both intuitive and empirical, and her insider's knowledge of all of the work that goes into a woman's seemingly effortless beauty never interferes with her willingness to succumb to the magic of the spectacle, which she knows simultaneously from the standpoint of the audience *and* the performer, the dazzled, credulous public and the sly, fleet-fingered magician.

She has assiduously corrected the gross errors of my disguise, functioning as the mother I never had to the daughter I never was. Once during one of our photo sessions she pointed out to me that holes ripped in the thighs of one's fishnets look sexy, slutty, calculatedly unkempt; but that holes ripped in the *feet* of one's fishnets, so that one's toes protrude like a hobo's, look destitute—worse, unhygienic—especially when, like my own horny yellow talons, the nails have been bitten down to the quick. How sweetly she explained to me that the errant straps of bras tantalize when they are thin and satiny but not when they are as wide as surgical dressings, like the thick elastic belts of my own matronly over-the-shoulder boulder-holders. She generously donated to me her pot of goo to salve my misshaven legs and taught me to walk in heels by placing one foot directly in front of the other, as if a policeman had just dragged me out of a swerving car and forced me to walk a straight line during a sobriety test. She has coached me on how to enlarge my lips by lining them one millimeter beyond their natural borders and she has waged a glamour jihad to force me to raise my eyebrows and make pouting Marilyn moues. Some women have Martha Stewart to help them become perfect homemakers; I have Amelia to help me become the perfect *tramp*.

Would that I had received more help from a store I visited recently. My desperate search for the perfect *wig* recently led me to an expensive Manhattan "salon" whose managers claimed that they had private dressing rooms and promised me when I called that they would let me try on what their catalogue describes as "haute couture for your head." I pictured a kind of Banana Republic for the bald, a place where I could browse at my leisure, snatch a few likely candidates off their Styrofoam stands, and then scurry away from public view into a closet in the back, there to contemplate in solitude the horror of my haggard masculine face framed by cascades of girlish ringlets. When I arrived, however, I found myself in a wig shop–cum–beauty parlor where a klatch of graying Jews sat chattering away about a terrorist incident in Tel Aviv in which two American tourists had been brutally gunned down by a member of Hezbollah, a horrific story made all the more macabre by the fact that the woman who was telling it was having her hair done and kept interrupting the incessant stream of gory details with which she entertained those around her to say "not too short on the sides there" and "a little more off the top, please. . . . The husband was crawling away and . . . what do you think, clip the bangs? . . . they shot him in the back. The wife . . . watch it when you spray me with that! . . . got it right between the eyes. She never stood a chance." In front of this gossipy platoon from the blue-rinse brigade, I announced to the clerk that I had come to try on women's wigs— "for drag," I enunciated clearly, thereby remaining true to my principles, at the expense, of course, of my self-possession, which gave way before—mice are said to frighten lions—that most harrowing of threats, a gaggle of old crones. The clerk acknowledged me with a curt nod and then made me wait an unconscionable length of time before she called a chic-if-expressionless girl who, with all of the ebullience of a mortician, took me into a booth adjacent to the main salon where she proceeded to explain the advantages of the luxurious pelts she laid before me, one after the next, in a voice that might easily have been describing tombstones and epitaphs, the advantages of marble over granite, sans serif over serif.

At least cheap wig shops let you see their products, even if they are as shapeless as raccoons scraped off a turnpike, but here I had to wait for her to bring out an uninteresting selection of their exorbitantly expensive stock. Worse, despite the promise of separate dressing rooms, I was afforded no real privacy but had to submit to another supervised "fitting" and hence to gaze upon that unearthly face in the mirror in the presence of another human being. Feebly, I tried to make light of the situation, but she was full of Semitic solemnity and refused even to acknowledge my pitiable attempts at humor but, clearly understanding my discomfort even if she made no effort to relieve it, simply raised one monitory hand, palm forward, and announced, "It's okay, it's okay." I suppose there was some compassion in her "okay" but I would much rather that she would have entered into the spirit of camp and laughed in my face outright than preside over the session with such cheerless Jewish fatalism, every movement I made an accusation, every refusal of every wig a twist in her side. Perhaps she was right to ignore my phony good spirits, although most people would have done me the favor of at least smiling at my gallows humor. I nearly purchased a $200 affair simply to buy an escape from the shop, but finally conjured enough presence of mind to tell her that I needed first to consult a friend, making a mad dash for the stairwell and sprinting down the steps two at a time.

Again, I wonder at the masochism that forces me to continue with this project. What do I hope to gain? It is as if I were not content with being candid about the many uncomfortable things that happen to me in my life but must seek out occasions in which my capacity for candor is tested, occasions in which it is nothing less than mortifying to be honest with others and with myself, occasions in which I must burst in to a group of old religious women and blurt out loud that I am a drag queen. My martyr complex leads me to meet my fate halfway, to select the wheel on which I would be racked, the pincers with which my eyes would be plucked, my nipples torn. I must be constantly testing myself, daring myself, goading myself on to new feats of self-torture. And what is this book but a test, an act of gratuitous heroism in which I am both the perpetrator of the crime and the judge who rectifies the injustice, in which I both tie the naked damsel to the rock and release her from her chains? I am an extremist, a self-flagellator delighted by every lash he gives himself. No one stands to gain from these excruciating escapades, and yet I persist in both committing the sins and dying for their expiation.

Him

Crucifixion is an apt metaphor for last night's date. A man excused himself after a few short minutes of chitchat, saying—several times in fact—"I don't want to waste your time, but you look nothing like your pictures." Humiliated, I opened the door for him, adopting a bored look as if to say, "If not you, then someone else," feigning elegant ennui, and then, as soon as I slid the bolt, collapsed into my chair virtually in tears, utterly defeated, my ennui giving way to a towering rage, trembling like Joan Crawford sacked by MGM. He was the second man I had seen to the door that evening. The first had arrived about ten minutes before and, thinking that it was my trick, I ushered him into the apartment where he gave me the once-over, from wig to stilettos, and said, almost breathless with dismay, "Is this Madelaine's apartment, 11G?"

When the man I had actually invited arrived moments later, he turned out to be a pipsqueak, well under 5'6" which meant that I loomed at least a foot above him in my heels, and he seemed taken aback when the door opened to reveal an all-star forward from the Women's NBA. What's more, I was experimenting last night with my new turbans, which I thought gave me a smart vintage look, like a flapper or a silent-movie heroine, and which perhaps he did indeed find quaint, if quaint is taken to mean old, something preserved in mothballs in a trunk, an archeological curiosity from the

Roaring Twenties. What made his premature departure worse was that he was terribly polite about leaving, although, by repeatedly rubbing my ugly visage in the discrepancy between my photographs and my actual appearance, he made me feel not only ugly but a swindler as well, a sexual grifter of sorts who had lured him to my apartment under false pretenses. Now that I think about it, he was not polite at all but terribly unkind and his courtesy was full of passive aggression, the resentment with which he heightened the impression of *his* integrity versus *my* deceitfulness.

My photographs are scarcely a month old and so, aside from the wrinkles around my mouth, which were given a Photoshop face-lift, look as much like Denial as possible, although perhaps, as in any photograph, confusions of scale are likely to occur, leading undiscerning men not to notice that I am a giantess until the door opens onto the Jurassic and a Tyrannosaurus rex in a bustier daintily extends in greeting its two-fingered forelimb. As critics have noted since the inception of the medium, the camera is also not the naked eye, but an editorial device. Moreover, those who know you only through photographs may be confused by the fact that backgrounds are never the same as they are in real life, costumes get dropped off at the cleaner to be replaced by unfamiliar outfits, and the time of day in which the picture was taken has an odd way of changing, as times of day often do. The Impressionists learned that the eye is never still, that the rigidity of gaze implicit in a painting by, say, van Eyck is a glorious fantasy, and the online cruiser experiences this basic visual truth over and over again in painful ways, his all-too-human flesh constantly being judged against the camera's ostensibly documentary fictions. Or at least this is one way of interpreting an event that may have a much simpler explanation, namely, that my visitor found me ugly, a hag, a ghoul.

Not long ago, another man bailed out as soon as he entered, following me into the living room, giving me the once-over, sniffing skeptically at the goods, and then concluding, with the smugness of someone well coached in the alibis of the human-potential movement, "I'm not feeling good about this right now," as if he were a housewife at a meat counter turning up her nose at something a little blue around the edges. I felt a twinge of relief when he left, having had sex only seconds before he arrived (the last man was still in the apartment when the buzzer rang and he carried out the door with him, on his boxer shorts, the better part of the makeup I had so carefully applied to my face), but I found this rejection mortifying nonetheless. I am growing increasingly impatient of the whole presumed purpose of this stunt—namely, sex—as anyone naturally would were he turned down with the kind of cold-blooded candor that I am, with men fleeing the apartment, their hair standing on end, as if they had just seen the Grim Reaper or the Headless Horseman.

I persist because of the book, not the booty, because the writing entertains me and gives my life structure, something that has been sorely lacking in the last year. Recently, I even went so far as to arrange dates with two relatively unattractive men for the sole purpose of gathering material, an extreme instance of the sort of intellectual opportunism that takes over when a writer caves in to the rhetorical needs of his story at the expense of his subject matter.

But as always happens when the scientist tries to confirm rather than test his hypotheses, my two laboratory guinea pigs refused to tap the levers of the right pellet dispensers, but simply curled up to sleep on the cedar shavings at the bottom of their cage. Absolutely nothing could get them to talk, and I found myself grilling them like an interrogator, asking if they were married, did they have children, could they tell me why they liked transvestites, did they like men as well, had they done this before, and so on, an inquest that elicited nothing more fascinating than "yes," "no," "I don't know," and "hard to say." There was something almost hilarious about the way I hung on their every word—all eight of them—probing and insinuating like a yellow journalist who catches the scent of a scoop, peppering them with questions in hopes that they would make some incriminating revelation, tell me some story of anguish, deliver up some choice tidbit of smut that I could weave into my narrative. But they just kept smiling and nodding, smiling and nodding, until I felt like grabbing them by the throats and screaming, "Tell me something that I can write about, goddamn it!" The fact that they remained mute as fish seems to me in retrospect almost-poetic justice for my prurience, a message from the muses that, the more greedily I lust after the comic or the sordid, the more fitful and banal the installments of material they would ration out to me.

Once again, Denial proves to be only an extravagant extension of Daniel. Throughout my career, writing has been bound up with the idea of myself as an exposer of falsehoods, a muckraker, a polemicist, and when Denial begins picking the brains of her unco-operative tricks, who find themselves put on the spot about fantasies they not surprisingly have difficulty discussing, she is adopting the inquisitorial techniques of her journalistic counterpart. Dressing in drag is something I have always done when I write; in order to investigate the way the Scientologists sell L. Ron Hubbard's books, I once pretended to be an excited fellow-traveler impressed by their marketing savvy, and in order to expose the fraudulent thinking of queer theorists rambling on about "gender liminality" and the "subversion of heteronormativity" on an e-mail Listserv, I posed as a tortuous French philosopher who enunciated to the group the pedagogic agenda of "orificial studies." Likewise, in drag I revert to the role of interviewer and attempt to exploit my position in order to pry out of my conquests the secrets of their complex desires. Drag, like all of the other lies I have told, has become a method of investigation, the journalistic tall tale I tell for the sake of the truth.

I am not the only one who tells lies. Last night a man I met online explained to me that he preferred drag queens to real women because the latter "play games" and want to talk about their feelings, while the former cut to the chase and "put out or get out." Women, he insisted, are cockteasers who string men along, break their hearts, and waste their time, making them jump through hoops just to get a little pussy, dithering about "should I or shouldn't I" in a way he contrasted to my own brash modus operandi. Of course, it was almost a foregone conclusion that he wouldn't show up for our date, and when I tried to e-mail him later that evening to complain about his lack of consideration, he had already blocked me from contacting him, possibly because, after whimpering about the capriciousness of the opposite sex, he realized that it isn't only women who string men along, waffle back and forth, hem and haw.

I try to imagine what it must be like for a man who is accustomed to being thwarted at every step, kept at arm's length, forced to navigate a minefield of inhibitions and timidities, suddenly to meet a woman who dispenses with all the romantic preliminaries and drags him headlong from first base to third before they even have a chance to break the ice with a few meaningless pleasantries. The effect must be like a pornographic film which presents a world free of female reservations, one in which the male will is never checked by his partner's diffidence but is nearly overwhelmed by the sexual ferocity of a strumpet as uninhibited as Fanny Hill. The world of pornography is an oddly homosexual world; what its spectators really want is to spend a recreational hour or two in a sexual utopia in which the relations between the sexes are governed by an exact symmetry of desire and women experience all of the recklessness and abandon of their male counterparts.

Denial is a denizen of this utopia, its queen. She meets men halfway, indeed, three-quarters to seven-eighths of the way, if not, in many instances, *all* of the way. She represents the opposite extreme of the shrinking violet and exhibits more eagerness than randy males, temporarily casting her pursuers in the uncharacteristic position of the pursued. What delights men about the drag queen is her sexual aggression, the ease with which she drops her drawers, stretches out supine beneath the bleachers like a delinquent high-school slut, and welcomes all comers. Men love her, in short, because she shares their impetuousness, their obscene lack of scruples, because she is—it should come as no great surprise—another male. In one sense, men who sleep with tvs and cds are often settling for a female effigy in the absence of the real thing; but in another, they actively seek out other men because they are exasperated by the contradictory expectations of the sexes, because they want someone as impatient as they are, as unrelenting in their pursuit of immediate gratification. My odd couplings with straight men may be more homosexual than I, who jealously protect my partners' virility—or at least my faith in it—care to admit.

Her

Women who behave like men may be appreciated for their aggression and lack of resistance, but ultimately they are not considered suitable girlfriend material, for the obvious reason that, as evolutionary psychologists explain it, their inseminators can never be certain if they are the fathers of their children, since during sex their sperm is simply dumped into a vat of collective jism. The infamous double standard is thus born: Men are allowed to be skirt chasers, but women can be promiscuous only at the peril of being attacked as fast and easy. My trick from the other night may have resented the way women toy with his affections, but it is unlikely that he truly admired or, more to the point, respected my own enthusiasm, that he thought of me as a "good girl," someone he could spend his life with, the specter of that vat of collective jism ultimately spoiling the bucolic picture of the quiet little house with the dog and the picket fence. In my life as Denial, I have been amazed to discover that, even as a part-time girl who slips in and out of her gender as readily as I slip in and out of my hose and heels, I cannot escape the liabilities of womanhood even as I enjoy its pleasures.

A case in point is an incident that recently occurred in the NYCShemale4male chat room. After I exchanged photographs with a handsome black man, I invited him over for sex, e-mailing him the detailed set of directions that I always have at hand explaining how to get to my apartment either by car or public transportation. These directions are so specific that they include a link to an online map indicating the location of my apartment building with a star, like the **X** that marks the spot of a pirate's buried, shall we say, booty. When he saw how remote my neighborhood is, he asked me to pay his cab fare, but I refused in high dudgeon, outraged by his unmanly cheapness. After declining his request in a flurry of angry private messages, a refusal that obviously struck a raw nerve, he returned to the public forum of the chat room and told everyone that "Silkysatindesire," my screen name for cruising, was such a trollop that she sends prospective mates prepackaged directions to her house, a service that suggests that every dog in the five boroughs of New York beats a path to her door in order to hump her like a bitch in heat. The men in the room howled with laughter, and I was made to feel like a nymphomaniac, amazed to find that, unlike "Jokersuperthug" and "Rockhardnqueens," who can cat around as much as they please, putting the make on every girl in the room, boasting about their stamina and the uncanny size of their dicks, I was expected to behave with becoming modesty lest my reputation, to the detriment of my sexual success, should suffer. It came as an enormous surprise to me that I could even acquire a reputation, so foreign is the curse of a bad name to a gay man, who operates on the unconscious assumption that, like any man, gay or straight, he will be admired for the number of conquests he makes. Suddenly, I was held to a whole new standard of behavior and I found myself aghast, if amused, by the injustice of the experience, once again reliving an abbreviated version of the women's movement. "Reputations" are campy anachronisms in my world, fictional liabilities that my gay friends and I are constantly laughing about, telling our promiscuous cronies that they will incur disgrace if they persist in their loose ways. How extraordinary to find one's feet held to the fire of such a preposterous superstition, an old wives' tale whose condemnation of me seemed as serious as if I had been accused, not of sending out maps, but of cavorting with goats in miters at black sabbaths or of sticking pins into wax dolls!

My unseemly forwardness can also be seen in my first AOL nickname as a girl, the chaste and tasteful sobriquet Deepdiksuk, the screen name I used until it ran afoul of AOL's Community Standards Board which determined that it violated the regulations governing "parental controls." I came up with Silkysatindesire by stitching together bits and pieces of the stage names of the other tarts in the NYCShemale4male chat room, who use such glamorous pseudonyms as HotNWldTigress, Exoticpanther, Pradagirl, MissLeopardXXX, TheLegendaryBabe, Sexxxychanel, Creamycoco, Theblackbarbie, SxRicanButterfly, Misbootylicious, Tigreskassandra, Velvetpanther, and Softnhotlips, titles that are often far more voluptuous than the shrews they refer to.

Such names suggest the kind of breathy, cheesecake femininity seen in the photo spreads in girly magazines which present airbrushed vixens smothered in marabou. And yet it takes only a minute watching innocent Christians mauled in this electronic Coliseum for all of these tigresses, panthers, and leopards to show their true spots. Their male aggression impishly peeps out from behind their gigantic implants. There is a 50 percent chance at any given moment that, as soon as you enter the room, you will find yourself embroiled in a catfight, a mud-wrestling match in which the real men—or at least the real men dressed in pants, not pantyhose—root for their favorite contestants, savoring the brutality of their kicks and scratches. Just yesterday, in the middle of an argument in which one girl was accusing the other of robbing her tricks and smoking crack, several smart-alecks began pretending that they were at a baseball game and started yelling for the hotdog vendor to bring them some popcorn and a Coke, saying, "Pass the brewskies," and shouting at an imaginary straggler blocking their view, "DOWN IN FRONT!"

One girl, Bronxcenterfold, a sexy Puerto Rican pre-op with luscious pouting lips who advertises herself as "DA MOST

BEAUTYFULL TS IN DA BRONX," makes it a point of
greeting girls new to the room by cackling maliciously over the
photographs they post on their Web sites, berating them in the
most unflattering terms, advising them to commit suicide and, as
she has told me on a number of occasions, "just go jump off the
Brooklyn brige." Once, I entered the room to find her gouging
the eyes out of a haggard, chalk-faced transvestite. I decided to
join the scuffle and take sides, praising the new girl as Helen of
Troy and criticizing "DA MOST BEAUTYFULL TS IN DA
BRONX" for her vulgarity and mean-spiritedness. She gave her
mutilated prey one last, teeth-rattling shake and, her mouth dripping with gore, turned her sights on me. Not surprisingly, the
men in the room leapt to her defense, largely in an effort to ingratiate themselves to a girl much more attractive than poor Denial,
who was forced to carry on alone, forsaken even by the faithless
transvestite, who allowed her champion to fend for herself as the
gutter-mouthed Centerfold showered her with a spate of obscenities. The men, in turn, consoled the stricken Centerfold with
assurances that I was angry because she was so much more beautiful than I was, as of course she is, but so full of bile, so gratuitously hateful, so addled by drugs and booze, that it surprises me
that men are willing to overlook her odious personality. I may be
far uglier than this swollen bladder of collagen and progesterone,
with her balloon lips and skintight pedal pushers, but when all is
said and done, I am far more feminine, if by femininity one
means kindness, a key component of femininity by most standards and one almost entirely absent from men who, appearances
to the contrary, are no more ladylike than drunken yahoos in
sports bars.

The NYCShemale4male chat room is a bitch-eats-bitch world
in which men, all men, both male and female, enter at their peril.
The male men are forced to grovel before the female men who
play hard-to-get with as much maturity and sophistication as
pubescent girls. They spurn the advances of their suitors with

puerile haughtiness, forcing them to ask permission to contact them privately and posting for the whole room to see the unsolicited compliments they are sent, as if by exposing these endearments to their classmates they had conceived a truly diabolical revenge, a reprisal that I am frequently at a loss to understand since the offensive remark is usually as impertinent as "you are beautiful" and "can I see you tonight, hot mama?" Because most of the girls in the room are escorts (out of necessity, I'm told, since they need extensive plastic surgery), many of the arguments that arise involve disputes over business transactions, as when a handsome eighteen-year-old Russian boy asked one of the snottiest divas if she had a sliding scale and would sleep with him for $5.00, all that he could afford. One would have thought he had been guilty of lèse-majesté and given the Queen of England a bear hug and a big wet sloppy kiss on the cheek, so loudly did the diva howl in protest, his faux pas quickly escalating into an international incident. Soon all of the girls in the room had entered the fray and he was forced to flee with his head between his legs as they hurled insults at him left and right, calling him a "cheapskate," a "tightwad," and a "nigger on welfare," an insult that led one hilarious black man to ask the offended girl if she took food stamps, Medicaid, or WIC.

The mercenary shenanigans in the room hark back to a pre–Sexual Revolutionary world in which no dates were dutch and men bore the cost, not only of the flowers and the dinner, but the diamond ring and the mink stole. The girls hawk their wares with cries as incessant as those of street vendors: "Gentlemen, generous gentlemen," "e$$cort/model here," "money talks, bullshit walks," "$eriou$ men only please," "I don't take freebies," and "can you pay my bills?" The sexual politics are as crude as those that governed the relations between the sexes during the 1940s and 1950s and girls lament the paucity of men "with fat wallets" who will take them on shopping sprees at Tiffany and Bergdorf Goodman, while the men, most of whom are not Rothschilds but penniless blue-collar workers, seem surprisingly modern in comparison, unwilling to be treated like Daddy Moneybags, occasionally even lashing out at the "whores" who seem to want them for one thing alone. Entering the room is like getting behind the wheel of a sexual time machine. The girls cultivate a nostalgically grasping femininity rarely seen outside of pulp novels and soap operas, posing as tantalizing houri out slumming. And yet at the same time that they are shameless gold diggers, they demand R-E-S-P-E-C-T and are enraged when dirty-minded brutes send them obscene notes requesting specific sexual favors, requests that they receive, not with the worldliness of hardened prostitutes, but with the quivering sensitivity of Victorian maidens. Girls charging $200 an hour for a "massage" and a "release" feign moral indignation at the venality of their tricks, most notably of married men, ostensibly because, while they themselves think nothing of posting photographs of themselves in scant swimsuits and plunging décolleté, they would never in a million years, heaven forbid, even think of violating one of the Ten Commandments. I suppose it is the fantasy of all whores that, at heart, they are really just convent schoolgirls.

But my fellow sisters can also be very funny when they relax, kick up their heels, remove their brass knuckles, and set aside their specious morality. Not long ago, a spontaneous discussion broke out about wigs after one of the older girls in the room facetiously announced that she was going to have a yard sale to get rid of some of her old pieces, whereupon a friend of hers claimed that these hand-me-downs were so "nappy" that you "could mop a floor with them" or scour "yur pots an pans." Suddenly it was girls' night out and everyone began to swap stories about wig disasters, much to the discomfort of the men, who remained tellingly silent during a gab session that perhaps revealed a little too much of the machinery behind their fantasies. One girl told a story about a man who, during oral sex, kept playing with her wig, raking his fingers through its curls, yanking on it even after she slapped his wrists and told him to "fuck off," claiming that she had just had her hair done and she didn't want it "mussed up." Since he refused to stop and didn't seem to realize that it was fake, she simply grabbed his hands in her own, pressed them to her skull, lifted her wig off and let go so that he was left actually holding it, free to tousle these synthetic "monofilaments" as much as he chose. She then took it from him and spread it out like a sleeping animal on the pillow beside them, telling him, when he exclaimed, "I thought you said that you just had it done," "I did, I just bought it." Another told how one very drunken evening, as she lay sleeping in the arms of her lover, her wig got caught in the metal band of his wristwatch and that both were so far gone that they didn't notice until the following morning when she awoke to find his (very hairy) arm flung across her implants.

On another occasion, in response to a girl's plaintive call "gentlemen, generou$$ gentlemen," I began calling out "gentlemen, de$$titute gentlemen," and the escorts in the room laughingly began lowering their prices in a kind of bidding war. They had descended to the low two figures when a beautiful black pre-op made her final offer and announced that she would do it for a Bud Lite and yet another for a Beef Chalupa at Taco Bell.

Him

I will always be able to answer the question "What were you doing when the lights went out during the big blackout of August 14, 2003?" I was sitting on the toilet in full drag performing an intimate act of hygiene in preparation for the imminent arrival of a gentleman caller, an NYPD officer who had warmed my heart (and, at the same time, chilled my soul) by sending me a photograph of himself pointing his pistol directly at the camera. The power went off at 4:10 and I was expecting him at 5:00, but when I saw that the stairwell was unnavigably black, I assumed that the deal was off and sat down in my recliner to enjoy my drink and a novel, slinging my wig across the back of a chair and removing much of my outfit. At 5:00 sharp, not a minute after, a door in the hallway banged open and slammed shut and a booming voice, reminiscent of Marlon Brando's in *Streetcar Named Desire,* screamed "DANI!" I hurriedly slapped my wig on my head and wrenched my fishnet body stocking up over my shoulders only to find my cop standing outside the apartment, winded and sweating, having scaled ten stories of stairs by feeling his way along the walls and counting the landings to get off on the right floor. It was an almost-heroic feat performed in my honor, not only because he was horny but because he needed to release some steam before heading straight from my bed to the station house, where he fully expected to be thrown into the trenches of whatever terrorist catastrophe was unfolding around us.

I was too unnerved by the ominous sounds of distant sirens and the honking horns of cars confused by the failure of the traffic lights to enjoy the sex, which seemed distinctly ill-omened, as if it were our last fuck, the last desperate gropes of a couple doomed to die before sunset, the twilight of Western civilization as we knew it. Afterward, my alarm continued to grow as he became more and more enraged about the blackout; but even as I felt frightened, I began enjoying the drama of the moment and acting the role of solemn Witness to Historic Events. He no sooner toweled himself off than he began railing against the Arab infidels, vowing vengeance for this mysterious atrocity, telling me how he felt that we should just go "nuke a country," kill Arafat, or appropriate all the Middle Eastern oil wells. He put his clothes back on as if he were dressing himself not in boxer shorts and a Hanes T-shirt, but in a full panoply of armor, while I sat on the edge of the bed, all lace and fishnets, my legs crossed, my brow knit in worry. I listened to his bluster like an anxious wife convinced that she would never see her beloved soldier boy again, imagining the worst, the knock on the door, the telegram, the meaningless military rhetoric extolling him as a hero who had died for the glory of his nation. As I saw him out, I pictured myself as in a photograph, waving good-bye with my hanky balled up in my fist, damp with my tears, and I said to him—the score began to swell—"You be careful now; I don't want to hear about any accidents." What an anticlimax it was when I sat down disheveled, my wig a mess, my clothes drenched in perspiration from the extreme humidity, a tragic figure sweating turbid rivulets of foundation, only to discover that it was not after all a preemptive nuclear strike by bin Laden, but a frayed cable in Rootstown, Ohio. But how we had enjoyed the little melodrama we improvised for ourselves, how exciting it was to waltz on the edge of that precipice!

Her

What remains in my memory after such encounters is everything except for the sex itself. Almost no lust remains in the dates I have with my tricks and if I am to respond at all (and most men—not unreasonably, one might argue—are very anxious that I do respond), I must take one third of a Viagra an hour beforehand. I no longer want to have sex with men, I now prefer the favors of a much more fickle lover, a Casanova far more mercurial in his moods, seldom flattering, often wounding: the camera, my nemesis. I am obsessed with my image, returning again and again to that defamatory mirror-mirror-on-the-wall in order to force it to change its mind, to rescind its judgment of me, to take back its libelous claims that the $2,000 I have sunk into cosmetics in the last year haven't done me a lick of good. I have taken hundreds of photographs since I began this project and of them maybe ten, purely by accident, present me in such a way that I am even marginally passable, and those are the ones snapped by the worst cameras, their focus an arty, painterly blur that obliterates wrinkles and softens contours in a way that no "anti-aging system" could possibly do. There is hope, yes, hope, and it comes, not from a bottle, but from a Kodak Funsaver, my own personal miracle "skin-remodeling wrinkle defense." I am engaged in a desperate search for the perfect photograph, a quest far more urgent—and, in many respects, far more frustrating—than my quest for the perfect heterosexual, who must now play second fiddle to my Olympus D-390. It is in the darkroom—not the bedroom—-where I have my rawest, raunchiest, sweatiest sex.

God knows my tricks must think I am hopelessly, pathetically vain, that I entertain myself by examining my face in the mirror and flipping through albums of my portraits, a reasonable conclusion, but one that must leave them feeling dismayed, since I clearly have nothing to be vain about. I recruit the men I meet online as my photographers, who, with the help of my new digital camera, indulge me by staging brief photo shoots, which they submit to perhaps because they think of them as my own peculiar form of foreplay, a prelude to sex, a warm-up exercise, a minor fetish in addition to my major one, or perhaps because they feel that they must humor an empty-headed girl who, like most women, is preoccupied with her appearance. Little do they know that, for me, far from being a *prelude* to sex, the photo shoots *are* the sex, and the sex itself is the *afterword,* the payment I make to my cameraman. I am not making love any more, I am harvesting my image. The exchange is not unlike that which occurs between a prostitute and her john, with the exception that no cash changes hands, only kisses in exchange for bytes. Even when they don't take pictures of me, I am still just harvesting my image in the sense that what I am really seeking from the encounter, what I am always looking for in their eyes, in their body language, in the way they talk, is a response to an unvoiced question: "Do you find me find me attractive, can you make love to me, how would you grade my disguise on a scale of one to ten?" How can I be a good lover when I have ceased enjoying sex and all that I am really attempting to achieve is a high test score?

Him

Last night I failed the test, dropped my pencil and walked out of the exam. I was talking to a swarthy man in his early twenties who professed never to have—to use his picturesque euphemism —"crossed over to the other side." He had been admiring my legs, praising my shoes, telling me how he loved my garters and fishnets, how when we met he wanted me to wear exactly that outfit, that see-through lace teddy with those red satin gloves and that black beaded choker, when he suddenly blurted out—cross my heart and hope to die—"Would you be willing to have sex with me with a bag over your head just so you wouldn't have to bother doing your makeup?" I am usually good about delivering stunning rejoinders when I am unfairly attacked, a talent enhanced by my typing speed, but this remark, inserted subliminally like a single bloodcurdling frame in a reel of film, caught me entirely off guard and I found myself speechless. I managed to say something cutting and then blocked him from contacting me, but he later e-mailed me an apology which I saved:

> i must say sorry about that it really was not conciderit but i will be conciderit when we get together. I am not experenced with such manners. what do you like? how can i make it good for you? let me know what your interestes are and how someone so inexperenced as myself can drive you

crazy. you are a lady a very sexy one who should have a younger man to treat her well. Jay.

Of course, I accepted his apology and even found myself laughing out loud when I responded, although I did have to tell him that his request to bag me up like a sack of groceries, notwithstanding his thoughtfulness in seeking to spare me the time and effort of putting on my makeup, wasn't exactly what a girl wants to hear from an admirer.

Her

Not that I don't hear it all the time from the photographs I take. I have entered into a duel with the camera, an affair of honor that I cannot win. And yet ridiculously I keep throwing down the gauntlet and challenging it to yet another round, bent on proving it wrong, on doing better, making it admit that, despite my age, despite my gender, despite my unmistakably male nose, square jaw, and increasingly pendulous ears, I am still desirable. I am mindful of Amelia's suggestion that I should cease harping on my ugliness, and it is true that no one, however empathetic, can sustain their interest in someone else's physical insecurities, especially when these insecurities are self-inflicted, the results of a game that, unlike the game of life, I was not born into against my will but chose to play. Again, I return to the image of my wooden leg. I never intended Denial to have feelings; she was a prosthesis for sex, nothing more. To my surprise, however, she is acquiring an inner life, she experiences pain, she feels shame about her looks, she gets excited about a new shade of eye shadow, she is proud when handsome men compliment her on her legs, and she is enraged when Internet bullies pull her pigtails and tell her that her face could stop a clock. Denial is becoming such a prepossessing figure in my imagination that she might, at least hypothetically, take over my life, and because I have no intention of letting this happen, I will kill her off sometime within the next year, amputate yet once more that severed leg that has somehow reattached itself, terminate the mad scientist's botched experiment, murder his Frankenstein.

The day before yesterday I took the worst photograph of myself I have ever taken, a watershed moment in the development of Denial's inner life. I have it in front of me on the screen. It is a picture of a middle-aged woman, in my eyes as desirable as one of da Vinci's caricatures, the famous lost "Duchess" perhaps, a greenish brownish thing that looks as if it had been marinating in the East River for the past six months. Her eyes are unspeakably evil, her expression joyless, the look of someone who religiously attends public executions, kills widowers she meets through lonely-hearts clubs, and pushes cripples in front of oncoming traffic. Half of her face—the lower half—is pigeon gray, while the upper half, where she ceased applying the pancake base in the hopes of achieving a more naturalistic effect, is mottled with copper streaks, greasy war stripes of MAC bronzer. Her lips are crimson and well-shaped, save for one corner of the upper lip where the gloss has bled slightly, making her look as if she had just ravened down something, not only raw, but alive; one suspects that, were she to open her mouth and burp, the feather of a parakeet might waft up and tickle her nose. She has not slept in fifty years, perhaps as many as a hundred; the bags beneath her eyes are not blue, they are black, while her lids are deep brown and the area just beneath the eyebrows an oily antique drab. Her hair has seen its better days and, while still thick, looks as soft as a Brillo pad, a fault for which she cannot be blamed since the officer who booked her refused to let her brush it before she was dragged from her cell in handcuffs and marched before the camera. She is not someone anyone would want to make love to, let alone eat at the same table with or, for that matter, ride in the same subway car.

I describe Denial in such harsh terms in order to accomplish several things. For one, I hope to make something amusing, even artistically appealing, out of something grotesque, to make a second likeness out of the first, show the laughter behind those evil eyes, correct her imperfections by endowing her with something I hold precious: self-awareness. In the course of my career as a writer, I have turned self-deprecation into an art form, a lifestyle, a type of therapy that I find far more "healing" than the useless ministrations of human potentialists who would have us "feel better" about ourselves, whereas I would have us feel—*worse*. In this sense, I am like penitential Lutherans and Calvinists who experience the pleasures of self-laceration and who find salvation in an awareness of their own insignificance, impiety, and wickedness. Embracing my flaws, flaunting them, leaves me feeling fearless and in control, liberated from the trammels of selfhood. I suspect that these are precisely the emotions that make Protestant religions so appealing to Holy Rollers. For me, drag is like old-time religion.

What's more, the insults I fling at this hag are a way of putting Denial in her place. They reestablish the natural hierarchy of our relations, a pecking order that this seditious dildo, this gaping-mouthed blow-up sex doll, is bent on subverting. She is my subordinate, my factotum, and when her insecurities and unhappiness begin to irritate her slave master, who has enough insecurities and unhappiness to last a lifetime, she must be turned over my knee and shown who is boss: not Uncle Tom but Simon Legree.

Perhaps I am so aggravated by Denial's insubordination because I am really not entirely convinced that she is worth this much trouble. Do I need the sex she provides me? Haven't I had enough, after some three or four thousand partners, to last several lifetimes? In truth, appearances notwithstanding, I am not a nymphomaniac. I don't need the sex I have and often wonder if I would be happier without it, if it weren't for the fact that, as I have mentioned already, sex provides me with a meager substitute for human contact in the absence in my life of real friendship. As a withdrawn, bookish misanthrope, I have never learned any more effective method of socializing than pulling my pants down and proffering to others my naughty bits. When Denial finally hangs up her falsies, how will I find the fleeting encounters that have provided me with companionship, with partners for the primate grooming rituals that are said to be so essential to the sanity of the higher apes who spend long stretches of their day de-matting each other's fur? Who will delouse my twelve wigs? Who will remove the leaves and twigs caught in my $25 Fulton-Street-Mall specials? When I am rid of her once and for all, I must create another sort of puppet, this one painted with a fixed smile of conviviality with which to attract both sexes, a gaping-mouthed blow-up doll intended, not for sex, but for camaraderie, for good fellowship. Denial is not the answer to the dilemma of menopause, she is a mere stopgap. A revolution far more radical than drag is called for if the recluse is to learn to live without the wild, orgiastic merrymaking of the whore.

Him

This disreputable alter ego brought me some unexpected
cameraderie just yesterday. As I was working online, an
admirer from California contacted me out of the blue simply to
tell me how beautiful I was and what a fantastic job I did with
my makeup. I protested modestly, with much bashful head-
shaking and demure fluttering of my hands, as if to say, "No-no-
no, you silly beast, stop flattering little old sickeningly repulsive
me," and he, of course, took the bait and set himself up as my
champion, defending me from myself, extolling my skills as a
makeup artist, my gorgeous figure, my natural good looks. His
compliments began spiraling out of control, and before I knew
it, he was offering to take me on an online shopping spree to buy
shoes, teddies, corsets, anything I liked, the sky's the limit—that
pair of leather boots? you've got it; that $150 wig? it's yours; that
set of Bobbi Brown makeup brushes? consider it done. One
minute, I'm sitting at my desk in my underwear and a coffee-
stained T-shirt writing an outline for an essay, and the next, I am
painting the Internet red with a perfect stranger, a mad spend-
thrift who, from our offices on opposite sides of the continent,
took me window-shopping at all the major online lingerie and
drag stores. His compliments made me giddy and the offer to
splurge was simply irresistible, and so I found myself led around
on a leash by a Daddy Warbucks bent on showing off his Midas

touch. It was a splendid electronic fantasy and such a hilarious non sequitur in the middle of my dull morning routines that I succumbed wholeheartedly, sweeping merchandise off the shelves into my shopping cart, pointing here, there, everywhere, as if I were some plutocrat's trophy wife striding through Saks in a mink stole, my loyal lackey trailing along behind me struggling under the weight of my purchases.

It came as something of a letdown when old moneybags said that urgent business called and that, rather than buy the things for me himself (we had drawn up quite a long list by this time), he would simply mail me a large check and that I could get whatever "my heart so desired," his sole proviso being that I send him a photograph of me wearing the fruits of his largesse. He told me that he would even FedEx the money to me so that I would have it first thing tomorrow, but tomorrow has come and is fast going and there is still no check in sight. I find myself at once amused and puzzled that I would waste thirty minutes with this man knowing all the while—I wasn't deceived for a second—that the chances of receiving a dime from him were nil. It was as if two strangers had met by accident and began spontaneously to "role-play," as they call it, to act out a sex scenario, much as some gay men play fraternity brother and rush-week pledge, and others play warden and inmate. Without warning, I found myself onstage playing the part of pampered sex kitten while he hammed it up as Aristotle Onassis, a clever skit we both found flattering, since I could be cosseted as the great beauty I decidedly am not and he could be admired as the sugar daddy he will never be. It is a little like Isak Dinesen's "Deluge at Norderney," in which two servants play the parts of their master and mistress during a devastating flood, only here we were being far less heroic, a bald man pretending to be a beautiful enchantress, a shoe salesman Bill Gates. The theatrical potential of the Internet is boundless, and I'm certain that Dinesen would have recognized and appreciated this unprecedented new way of lying and, given her own penchant, indeed, her gift, for telling fibs, may even have parked herself in a chat room and tried to pass herself off as Pavarotti or the Duke of Windsor.

On the subject of role playing, I had sex the other evening with a rather peculiar fetishist who asked me to put on my lipstick while he watched, a not-uncommon fantasy and one that I could easily fulfill. Foolishly, however, when he requested that I put on the sexiest lipstick I had, I brought in a mirror, my lipstick brush, and a dollop of cherry red pigment smeared on a palette, not thinking that what he wanted to see was not me showing off my esoteric makeup techniques, but something much more mundane, me massaging my lips with a suggestive retractable tube, drawing on big wet loops of whorish red. Instead, I treated him to a show-and-tell like some unsteady fashion student painstakingly demonstrating a lesson she had only recently learned, drawing on a Cupid's bow with her lip liner and then filling it in like a shape in a coloring book with pedantic, unpracticed concentration. Needless to say, he looked quite bewildered, a response that registered both on his face and between his legs.

He next requested something else that men often want me to do: smoke cigarettes while they masturbate. Here, too, I'm afraid I was something of a disappointment. He handed me a brand-new pack still in its plastic wrapper and since I was wearing my elbow-length Lycra gloves, which are not very gracefully removed, the fingers tending to invert like latex dish-washing mitts, I was forced to grab a corner with my teeth and rip it open, a move I attempted to perform with a sort of sultry ferocity, staring challengingly into his eyes as if daring him to object. Once the pack was open, however, I couldn't pry the cigarettes out and ended up simply poking ineffectually at the filters. Since this was clearly getting nowhere and I was losing face by the second, I began whacking the pack against the palm of one hand, again trying to look smart, chic, suave, cool as a cucumber, again staring into his eyes challengingly, feeling like someone in a play who has forgotten his lines and who tries to bluff his way through the awkward silence by means of sheer stage presence, sheer cheek, and audacity. Finally, he did the gentlemanly thing for this poor damsel in distress and removed one for me, but he failed to carry through on the gesture and light it, merely handing me a pack of matches which of course I could not easily tear off, my fine motor skills once again impaired by the Edwardian formality of my attire. After several unsuccessful attempts, I managed to squeeze one between my fingers, but so close to the head that I felt certain that my gloves would catch fire and melt before my very eyes, a concern that made me drop the lit match onto the parquet floor. Once I returned to the sofa and got my cigarette lit, I sat back like a movie star, crossed my long lovely legs, took a lazy, languorous draw, and then flung my hand back with marvelous elegance and sophistication, projecting glamorous apathy while he masturbated furiously. I intended to blow out two cinematic curls of blue smoke, but just as I began to exhale, my virginal lungs felt the scorching heat of the tar and nicotine and I erupted into hacking convulsions, wheezing and sputtering, my head sinking between my legs, giving way to a noisy seizure of stertorous snorts that destroyed any semblance of the bitchy savoir faire I had hoped to convey, to say nothing of wrecking my disguise, since my breathy whisper suddenly gave way to the ferocious roar of a wounded animal. He was too busy with his own fantasies to thump me on my back, past caring about my coughing fit, and by the time I could breathe again, it was his turn to be gripped by spasms. I seriously doubt that I will see him again but he did leave behind the cigarettes, which I will use as props in my self-portraits, although, like Clinton, I will make certain next time not to inhale.

Her

And self-portraits are now my preeminent concern. A disturbing pattern is emerging in my daily drag routines. I come home from the gym, do my makeup, and then take as many as 50 to 150 photographs of myself, which I carefully review before I go online to cruise. Not only is this obsession drastically reducing the amount of time I spend online and hence the amount of sex I am having, but almost invariably the photographs are so ghastly that I lose heart and cannot bring myself to invite a man over, knowing full well the calamity that awaits him. As the evidence of my hideousness mounts in shot after shot, my libido goes into deep-freeze and I long for a respite from the war, a quiet evening with my novel, hunkered down in the trenches, far away from the fatal explosions of the flashbulb.

The stakes of the game were recently ratcheted up a notch when, after receiving in the mail two beautiful new wigs, which I had purchased weeks before off the Internet, I took several dozen photographs that appeared to me truly magnificent, poster-girl pretty, especially the close-ups of me wearing a piece that Wigsalon.com identified as "Maggie," "a daring fashion statement" that is "new and truly unique from Rene of Paris" (unlike the somewhat more severe "Karen" which, even though it was listed in the store's "medical collection," was also from the House of Rene, a designer boutique that apparently caters to the chemo crowd). Delighted with my new photographs, I immediately posted them on my Web site and bravely strode into the NYCShe-male4male chat room, fully expecting to receive a standing ovation, only to be greeted by a drunken transsexual named Almondjoy who began berating my appearance as if there were no noticeable improvement in my looks from the old photographs to the new. Carried away by her own cleverness, she turned from my face to an appraisal of, as she sarcastically called my outfits, my "designer clothing," my $2.99 fringed shawl purchased at a closeout store, my gold Lycra evening gloves, their tips stained with lipstick from pulling them off with my teeth, and my beaded choker (in fact, a hairband I bought on sale, two for one). She concluded her autopsy by saying that she felt that she was in an m4m room (i.e., male for male), and I replied by saying that I felt I was in a d4d room, drunk for drunk. Although this has happened countless times, I am continually surprised by the cruelty of these anonymous cads who hurt me far more than I care to admit, although, I am happy to say, never without paying a price for their dastardliness, however small.

Almondjoy's drunken rant sent me into a photographic tailspin and every night for weeks now I have been snapping away trying to recover the excitement of that first set of deceptively flattering photographs. My vanity was so wounded by her assault that, out of perversity, in an act of self-mutilation, I e-mailed the lurid mug shot I had taken days before to a straight man who had been pestering me for a blow job, asking him if he still wanted to have sex with me now that he knew what I really looked like, an inhuman thing who was not even passable as a male, let alone as a female. To my amazement, his ardor did not cool, and the barrage of messages from him continued unabated, behavior that perhaps reveals a predilection on his part for molting orangutans in their golden years.

I transmute the pain of my life into anecdotes which I offer for the amusement of others. In this way, I reap social rewards from things that would otherwise simply diminish me. Through self-deprecation, I spin out tales that make others laugh at my weaknesses and at the same time admire my candor. I wage a merciless campaign of self-awareness in which I exchange my humiliations for social respect. The victim becomes the humorist and thereby makes his defeats victories, his tragedies comedies, the things that shame him the sources of his pride. My compulsive self-deprecation is a form of unilateral disarmament that puts my audience at ease and compels them to see the buffoon in another light, that of an intrepid explorer of the self, a heroic figure and not the pusillanimous lunatic who stars in the embarrassing anecdotes he tells. And what is this book but one long amusing anecdote, one long comic routine in which I entertain my readers by presenting myself in the worst possible light, a light that over time becomes distinctly flattering, casting over its protagonist a kind of glory that motivates me to perform more and more reckless feats on the high wire of self-discovery?

Him

My photographs have not curbed my need for sex. Yesterday I was in a perfectly swinish mood and had three anecdotes within the space of four hours. The first was a dull, stolid, incommunicative Mexican (in fact, the orangutan-lover, who I felt deserved to be rewarded for his persistence and much-appreciated lack of discrimination). The two that followed, however, made up for his reticence and jabbered incessantly. The first of these was a redneck from Bay Ridge, who reeked of cigarette smoke, which permeated everything from his T-shirt to his pubic hair. After very mechanical sex, he launched into a diatribe against his "evil cunt of an ex-wife," his fat fifteen-year-old daughter whom he refused to leave alone for even a few hours for fear that she would get herself knocked up like the rest of the "bitches" in her family, and his "goddamn mother-in-law from hell," an evil shrew whom he said he wanted to push out of an airplane at 30,000 feet and then dive very quickly so that he could smile at her from the cockpit the instant before she splattered on the pavement. Listening to his apoplectic tirade, I felt that I had entered the conversation in medias res, that I was being swept along on the brisk current of his stream of consciousness, which eddied around me, swirling with rage and a fierce sense of inexplicable grievance. He spilled his guts out without for a second even wondering—worse, even caring—if I were interested in being submerged in this avalanche of intestines.

Instead, as seems to be my lot in life, I was the victim of yet another emptying, a voiding of bile, and my role in the exchange was to sit still like a porcelain chamber-pot and let myself be filled to the brim with the excretions of someone else's life.

Next in line was a handsome Puerto Rican Web designer with a much more attractive personality but an even greater tendency to run at the mouth, despite the fact that, in order to escape the onslaught of nonsense, I performed my best cigar-store Indian impersonation. I went into hibernation, as if I were an animal sensing danger, trying to blend into the complicated patterns of the bedspread covering my futon sofa, like a chameleon sitting on a leaf. He told me that he was usually shy and taciturn but that he was relaxed with me and so he felt free to release the lake of words that both his frustrated relations with women and a crippling stutter had dammed up inside. Unlike my previous visitor, he did not regale me with the palace intrigues of a fractious Italian dynasty, but chose instead to impress me with his wisdom and transform me into his naïve and obedient disciple crouching at his footstool, a role that women must assume all of the time but that offended my intellectual machismo. There I sat while he rewrote all of Confucius and the Kabala, tossing off such conundrums as "if you t-t-t-take someone apart, you have t-t-t-t-to put them b-b-b-b-back together again" and "you've g-g-g-g-got to make sure that you are in the right mind space and not l-l-l-let the outside world come into that space and m-m-m-make it another kind of space you didn't intend it to be." He was so delighted with my servility that he described our presumed marriage of minds as an impromptu philosophical summit in which "I'm coming from my world and you're c-c-c-coming from yours and we sit down and we create a m-m-m-mind space in which we both share a little bit of your space and a little bit of m-m-m-mine." More yours than mine, I thought to myself. In fact, all yours, none of mine.

Such encounters highlight for me the painful contradictions of my sex life, contradictions that exactly parallel the contradictions found in the fantasies of women living in the age of emancipation. On the one hand, I enjoy the pleasures of submission, enjoy being part of the flock of human cattle shepherded along by the tribe's alpha males, a satisfaction that must have evolutionary roots in the physical security our ancestors found huddling together around the campfire, forming protective packs that maintained their cohesion only if leaders emerged to impose on them a hierarchy of power, a pecking order that prevented fragmentation by assigning each member a specific function. The heterosexual couple is a microcosm of the flock, a miniature herd guarded by its own watchdog, and the passive partner experiences the exquisite comfort of knowing she is guarded, that no harm can come to her so long as her protector remains by her side, keeping at bay predators who roam the dark and hostile universe lurking beyond the perimeters of the campsite.

But the satisfactions of passivity never wholly eclipse the pleasures of power. Leaders emerge for a reason: they eat better, have more mates, therefore more offspring, and everywhere they turn are awarded respect. Few people experience the delicious security of being subordinate to a stronger guardian without at least speculating about the privileges of power, and the consequence is that every bottom is a latent top, while every top longs to relinquish his supremacy and assume a lowly but sheltered position within the pack, a yearning for surrender that explains the S/M fantasies of the high-powered CEO who is as authoritative in the boardroom as he is docile in bed. When I am forced to sit as patiently as a rock while waves of words wash over me, I see clearly how my sexual passivity must contend with my desire to dominate and control others, a conflict that women are experiencing more keenly as their traditional role as domestics collapses and they assume their places in the increasingly androgynous hierarchies of power that now prevail in the modern workplace.

Her

E xcept, that is, at the cosmetic counter, where the hierarchies of power are distinctly matriarchal. Recently on one of my regular excursions to Sephora, my makeup Mecca, I was befriended by one of their "artists," an attractive fifty-year-old woman who, as it turns out, lives right around the corner from me. She expressed interest in the project and volunteered to drop by and watch me put on my makeup, correcting me along the way, and then, after she had erased any glaring booboos and added a number of glamorous touches of her own, to take photographs of the resulting masterpiece. For four hours, this cosmetic perfectionist poked, prodded, and powder-puffed my face. She highlighted and contoured, stippled and spritzed, tweezered and bronzed, and then finally, after an exhausting afternoon of nose-to-nose scrutiny, she laid down her brushes. The moment of truth had arrived, my brand-new face was about to be revealed (like the radiant visage of a once-disfigured actress in an old Hollywood film), the glass was held up before me, and I looked deeply into the eyes of . . . dowdy Aunt Hortense, a septuagenarian spinster residing in an assisted-living facility in the Bronx. Four hours of painstaking work, so generously donated by my forbearing neighbor to the cause of my fabulousness, had turned me into a frump, a mannish old maid in support hose and orthopedic shoes who scatters bread crusts to pigeons in the park. The slight-if-untenable semblance of glamour that I had managed to create with my own ham-handed daubs was effaced by my neighbor's naturalism, her uncannily successful attempt to make it appear as if I were wearing little or no makeup, as if I had just risen from my bed, dewy fresh, chastely nude, a vision of unaffected simplicity. Gone was the aged vamp, the dissipated madam of a high-class brothel, a well-heeled procuress with her own seedy elegance, and in her place was the ill-tempered night nurse of the county old-folks' home.

It is a truism of modern makeup that less is more, that the thousands of potions available on the store shelves are intended to enhance our beauty—not create it—and that hours must be squandered hiding the traces of our labors, concealing the concealer. This aesthetic of understatement is incompatible with the whole phenomenon of drag, which is not about enhancement, about the subtle augmentation of an aquiline nose or an enviable set of eyebrows, but about enshrouding the face in a second skin, a mask made of talc, corn silt, and silicon. Drag makeup is white-out. It is about distraction, about creating a visual disturbance on the face, a riot of color so loud and assaulting that the viewer falls for the ruse and stares in wonder at the commotion rather than contemplating the obvious inadequacies of the disguise.

My friend from Sephora, working on the premise that only bad girls wear their makeup on their sleeves (I wear mine on my collars, dresses, gloves, you name it), misunderstood the nature of the challenge involved in feminizing the male face, an error rooted in the dour moralism of the contemporary aesthetic of naturalism, the prudish fear of cosmetics as satanic maquillage. Naturalism is a puritanical aesthetic infused with a Victorian priggishness that would have its cake and eat it, too, allow its proponents to maintain their ladylike primness and yet indulge in the irreligious narcissism of painting themselves. In fact, the new naturalism is so sanctimonious that one of the appeals of drag makeup to heterosexual men is that it breaks the taboo against ostentatious, highly stylized makeup and thus signals to its admirers that they are looking at a bad girl misbehaving, someone who shows her makeup like loose women once showed their ankles or knees. I owe many happy hours in the bedroom to my more understated sisters whose cowardliness and caution enhance the seductive effect of my cosmetic heresies.

The other evening I found myself embroiled in another catfight with a decidedly overstated girl who shares my philosophy of makeup, the vicious Bronxcenterfold, "da most beautyfull ts in da Bronx," whose strategy of self-promotion as a hooker is to disparage the competition, whom she attacks for having fat asses and asymmetrical implants. Once again, she started in on my photographs, my ugliness, my masculinity, the fact that I was a man in a dress ("so are you," I reminded her), that "you are waring yur wive's clothes," and that she had heard that there was a position open for a 600-pound tiger to replace the one that attacked Roy Horn in Las Vegas. Of course, I was angry, but as my faith in humanity—at least the malignant version of it that one finds on the Internet—diminishes, I am somewhat less surprised by the malice surging beneath mankind's latest human-rights atrocity, the chat room.

I sparred with her for a few minutes and then asked if she had seen the paragraph I had written about her in my diary, now posted on my Web site. At first, she was incredulous and scoffed at me but, when I finally convinced her that I had indeed discussed her behavior, she seemed almost pleased to have made enough of an impression on an author to be included in his book. When she couldn't find my site, however, she became increasingly desperate, giving way to her curiosity in an undignified way and begging me to tell her what I'd said. I posted the Web address for the room and, when she still couldn't find the reference, even though I gave her a specific page number, I asked her if she would like me to type the concluding sentences of the passage and, without waiting for her permission, promptly did so:

She is . . . so full of bile, so gratuitously hateful, so addled by drugs and booze, that it surprises me that men are willing to overlook her odious personality. I may be far uglier than this swollen bladder of collagen and progesterone, with her balloon lips and skintight pedal pushers, but when all is said and done, I am far more feminine, if by femininity one means kindness, a key component of femininity by most standards and one almost entirely absent from men who, appearances to the contrary, are no more ladylike than drunken yahoos in sports bars.

Throughout our little tiff, the room had remained silent, possibly because, as the sole cross-dresser in attendance, I am viewed with distrust, if not open contempt, and also because no one wants to set themselves up as da most beautyfull ts's next victim and watch horrified as their imperfections are aired in public before a tactless tribunal of foulmouthed rivals. To my great satisfaction, da Bronx was too stunned to respond and when she finally did manage to fight back, was so agitated that her spelling—never her best feature—disintegrated into an incoherent stream of insulting, if only vaguely recognizable, expletives which culminated in "I will have you burned at the steak!" "Ribeye or porterhouse?" I inquired and then announced, as was indeed the case, that I needed to respond to a few men whom I had neglected during our squabble and who looked like promising candidates for my hand on this chilly fall evening.

Can it be that after a lifetime of skepticism about the intelligence and integrity of my fellow man, I am still so naïve that I am surprised by cruelty? Quite honestly, it flabbergasts me, makes no sense whatsoever, confounds all of my beliefs. I can, of course, imagine thinking to myself "silkysatindesire is one hell of an ugly bitch" but I simply cannot imagine approaching Ms. Desire and telling her to her face how repugnant she is, let alone before a room of thirty-six other people who, rather than gasping in astonishment at the barbarity of the outrage, join in the laughter and begin itemizing her deformities feature by feature. It is not an exaggeration to say that I am shocked by this primitive schoolyard bullying, this boorish sadism worthy of uncivilized fifth-graders.

In the defense of men who are, in most respects, completely indefensible, the girls in the NYCShemale4male room have been degraded by the mockery that they themselves have received, derision that, contrary to my idealistic beliefs, does not strengthen moral fiber but pulverizes it, tears it down, makes them want to turn the tables and feel the rush of power their hecklers feel as they chase them through the streets or taunt them from their cars. What's more, these are men who, for very good reason, are acutely self-conscious about their bodies and are thrilled when they find others who have been less successful than they are in the whole makeover game. Another contestant's deficiencies bolster their confidence in their success, which is plausible only relatively speaking, when placed next to someone else's failure, not in relation to the standard of plausibility provided by real women. Perhaps this is why I am so reviled in this room: because they actually need me, need someone who isn't passable, a spectacular mess who makes their own mess a little less—spectacular. In this sense, I am doing these girls a favor by providing the room with the "before" picture to their glorious "afters," the hair-raising "don'ts" to their voluptuous "do's."

And yet it is the very nature of online interaction, and not the insecurities of its participants, that accounts for most of this inhumanity. The chat room is a psychological and social limbo. On the one hand, it has a quasi-physical reality in that it consists of a collection of real individuals sitting in real rooms, however widely dispersed. On the other, since we can't see those with whom we are conversing, since they are only icons on the screen, and since we in turn are an icon ourselves and will remain anonymous unless we choose to disclose our identities, as I have done, our interlocutors do not really exist, can't retaliate, can't strike back, and are in a sense not really there at all but are just pixellated wraiths and therefore easy targets. The chat room creates the conditions for a kind of collective epidemic of Tourette's, a thinning of the membrane that divides internal dialogue from public dialogue, our thoughts from our actions. Aside from the sandbox, it is one of the few public realms in which we give free reign to the narcissistic caprices of the Id, partly because anonymity provides such a cozy refuge for scoundrels, and partly because the chat room, so subjective in form, so invisible, is easily mistaken for our own consciousness where nothing is censored, nothing repressed, and everything can be uttered with impunity.

As I have mentioned, I am afraid to abandon Denial altogether because her promiscuous encounters fend off the solitude that would otherwise engulf me. But there is a way in which the antics of my whorish sister only intensify the isolation of her reclusive brother. Denial is the phantasmal denizen of one of the most antisocial inventions of our time, the Internet. The Web is not an "online community," as it has been romanticized, but simply a network of other isolated monads living in a world that computers have helped fragment even as their apologists tout their ability to bring us all together, to unify the far-flung corners of the globe into one tiny electronic village. The "online community" is less a bustling town hall where strangers meet and connect than a honeycomb of cells in which shut-ins rap out messages in code. My computer has become a ball and chain imprisoning me in my apartment. It has made me more, not less, homebound. It does not create "community," it creates lives of parallel solipsism, atomized lives divided by a medium that deprives us of fresh air and keeps us trapped in our desk chairs, reluctant to pursue face-to-face encounters with neighbors who have dwindled into flickering ciphers on phosphorescent screens. Denial both brings people into my life and keeps them out. She is at once my bawd and my bodyguard, throwing me into intimate relations with strangers and yet holding them at arm's length. The Internet is a symptom of my reclusiveness, not its solution.

Him

ast night I met a fellow solipsist who had actually read the first
hundred pages of this diary. He said that he had downloaded it
and enjoyed it immensely, that he thought I was "a hoot," and even
referred to passages that he had found particularly amusing, thus
proving to me that he had indeed read it (he promised, for instance,
that, if we ever met, he, as a black man, would refrain from asking
me at the door for his customary fee, a loan of $5.00). I asked him if
he would be willing to get together for a drink to discuss his own
interest in transsexuals and he readily agreed, even though I
warned him that I thought he was so handsome (he had sent me his
photograph) that I might be forced to make a pass at him and that if
I did he should accept my apologies for my bad behavior in advance.
He wanted me to dress in drag so that he could "get the full effect"
and I, in turn, asked his permission to forgo my "little voice" for the
evening, since I could not imagine interviewing this obviously
bright person while speaking in my falsetto, the aspect of my disguise that constrains me most, like bound feet—in my case, a tied
tongue. As it turned out, we got very high from the potent marijuana he brought and barely skirted the subject of his sexual interests, but instead practiced them without my even needing to pounce.

I was surprised that he wanted to have sex with me after reading
all of the atrocious things I have written about myself here, but he
was undeterred and he left me feeling, if not beautiful, then a little

less repulsive, a gift that any girl wants from a man and one that, it goes without saying, she will treasure far more than flowers or chocolates. How could he possibly have been interested in fucking me? My diary is so cold and clinical, an antiaphrodisiac likelier to suppress desire than arouse it. The fact that my visitor could get it up for this biological mutant terrorizing the male population of metropolitan New York honestly amazes me and I feel a little awed by the indiscriminate nature of the male libido, so ruthless in its will to pleasure. Moreover, I was concerned that he would view my cross-dressing as a practical joke (which, of course, it is in a way), and that the disclosures I make about my own lack of interest in women's clothing would make him feel misled, even mocked; but if this is the case, he was quite willing to submit himself to the swindle. I found this puzzling, since it should be very obvious from reading my stories that I am an opportunist and not a fetishist, that I wear garters and heels much as hunters wear olive drab—not because they actually want to *be* vegetation but because they want to get as near as possible to their prey.

During pillow talk, he told me about his former wife, who died tragically in a car accident in 1995. They had been married for five years, a scam since she was a transsexual and could not be legally married to another man. He said he had loved her deeply, that she had always "watched my back" and been fiercely loyal to him even when he didn't "have two cents to rub together," idioms that (I'm not sure why) somehow revealed how keenly he missed her. After her death, overwhelmed by grief, he confessed to his sister that his wife had been a man and she admitted that she had always suspected as much solely on the basis of her height, 5'11''. What's more, his sister was not unacquainted with gender confusions of her own. Her first husband had been a homosexual, apparently quite a promiscuous one who disappeared for long unexplained absences and once at Halloween had dressed in drag, a costume that "kind of stuck" and that launched his career as a cross-dresser, a pastime that eventually led to the breakup of their marriage.

Ever since I came out at thirteen, I have avoided keeping secrets of the magnitude of my date's, adhering to the belief that furtiveness, lying, covering up, eventually undermine one's peace of mind and that only by being true to oneself can one live an honorable life. Since then I have had many reasons to question this precept, even though I have never successfully challenged it, as should be obvious from the candor I attempt to achieve in my books, the protracted confession that I did indeed chop down the cherry tree, to say nothing of laughing about the pubic hairs on the Coke can and snapping the thong of Monica Lewinsky. But however emotionally debilitating I find lying, it does have one advantage: It produces the conflicts from which good stories are made.

For someone with as inflexible a sense of self as I have, drag has allowed me to expand my range of possibilities, to play another character in another life. It allows me to soften recalcitrant aspects of my personality, a therapeutic exercise for a man who thrives on repetition, who buries himself in deep ruts, and rarely deviates from rigid habits almost entirely insusceptible to change. And yet as I try to make myself more resilient and achieve a degree of uncharacteristic fluidity, I find that in most respects I simply will not liquefy. What's more, I harbor moral reservations about the whole act of liquefaction. I will never be able to experience the full liberation of this Keatsian experiment in negative capability because I cannot wholly let myself go, turn my back on that vast edifice of habits in which I have confined myself for decades, a structure almost architectural in its vastness and, while to all appearances austere and inhospitable, is all I really have to call "home."

Even my drag persona is marked by my inability to change. The reason that Joan Crawford remains lodged in my face is that she is the only way I can transpose my real personality into someone of the opposite sex without losing touch with everything that defines me. My persona as a woman must emanate masculine self-possession, must not compromise the intellectual imperiousness I project in my daily interactions with people, as it would were I to adopt the giddy mannerisms of Marilyn Monroe or one of her contemporary epigones, a Melanie Griffith or a Jennifer Tilly. What's more, as a good old American crank devoted to the high-religious principles of individuality, I am temperamentally unsuited to the campiness of masquerade and my performances are therefore always hamstrung by my righteousness. My venture into acting is at best a halfhearted affair that involves, not the wholesale invention of a new feminine personality, but a compromise with a Daniel Harris who views the lie of drag as a form of self-betrayal, disloyalty to my hard-won integrity, an illegitimate effort to be something I am not.

Her

Which is not to say that I am content with what I am. I have not had sex as a gay man in many months, perhaps as long as a year. At least twice I have gone to the Brooklyn park in my ethnic neighborhood to cruise, but after wasting an hour or two drooling over gay black men (who are as coy, if not more so, than their fickle white counterparts), I left in a huff, disgusted by their self-defeating finickiness (most often totally unjustified), as well as by my own acute awareness of my age and lack of sex appeal. I am no longer confident that I could attract a gay man, whose standards are altogether higher than the sex-crazed fetishists I meet online. Besides, I am really not sure what gay sex would feel like any more, so estranged am I from the whole scene and so incapable do I feel of luring a man with my actual body and my real, unpainted face, rather than with the inveigling enticements of a spackled mannequin in mail-order lingerie. In the past, during long depressions, the reawakening of my libido was one of the first signs that the clouds were lifting, that the terrible numbness was easing, that I was finally able to move my sleeping limbs, still tingling with pins and needles. Lust has often been the route I have taken back to the world, the way I dispel the shadows of self-preoccupation, escape the torments of my inner demons, remind myself that I am alive. Now when I am out on the streets, I feel disembodied, transparent, an invisible man. What defines this void, gives it shape, allows it to be seen, are my costumes, much as H. G. Wells's protagonist assumed a discernible form only when he was wearing a felt fedora and sunglasses. Likewise, I, too, have quaffed the mysterious "decolorizing" formula and now have legs only when I zip my knee-high black boots up over my calves, a torso only when I hook the crotch of my teddy, and forearms when I pull on my elbow-length evening gloves.

The loss of any sexual connection with the world and the decline of the myriad opportunities I once had to flirt, show off, ogle others, and be ogled in turn, have intensified my feelings of isolation. Unseen, unadmired, I feel terribly alone. I experience my solitude not only when I am in my apartment, but when I am standing amidst crowds, brushing against people who might as well mistake me for a lamppost or a parking meter. Only when the void that I have become is covered in drag do I become visible again, an object to be admired by men whose lascivious stares confirm my existence, something that my isolation all too often leads me to doubt. Losing contact with my homosexuality and with other homosexuals is disembodying me, rendering me incorporeal, turning me into a ghost about whom it could be legitimately said, as it was about Wells's hero, "That's not a man at all. It's just empty clothes."

As I experience these things, I become acutely conscious that my very sense of selfhood is contingent on others, not only on the impressions they formulate of me, but on how my actions impinge on theirs. When people cease to make these impressions, they feel a distinct sense of vanishing, a slow fadeaway into extinction. I am increasingly terrified by this endless social dematerialization. So much of my unhappiness stems from the absence of response to both my body and my work. I no longer know who or what I am, how I fit into the structure of my society, what conceivable use I have for others, what place I occupy or function I serve.

Often when I am reading or struggling to write a sentence, I enter a chat room without intending to meet anyone and remain there for hours, occasionally answering the instant messages I receive only to return absentmindedly to the task at hand. College students living in dormitories often leave their doors ajar, not wanting to preclude social interaction entirely, but seeking to keep open some channel of communication, to maintain some dim, distant awareness of the goings-on of the herd, to attend to the sounds of huddling animals, feel their body heat, smell their reassuringly familiar odors. The same impulse lies behind the need some people feel to keep the television on at all times droning away in the background, providing a constant reminder of the presence of others within one's vicinity, grazing in the grass by one's side, just on the other side of the TV screen and the monitor. Evolutionary biologists would probably say that we originally needed such reassurances in order to receive the warnings the tribe issues when an attack is imminent and to react swiftly and in a coordinated fashion to predators. It is strange to think that thousands of years after hunting and gathering, I still feel this deep-seated need for the background murmur of social interaction and that my ears are still attuned to any sounds of collective unrest or excitement. When we lose touch with these sounds, when we straggle off down the wrong path and find ourselves foraging alone, we naturally feel afraid, defenseless, unprotected. The diminishment of self I constantly experience in my loneliness is rooted in my loss of contact with the pack, whose whereabouts is now unclear to me, thereby heightening my feelings of vulnerability. Loneliness is not just isolation, it is also fear.

Him

I recently encountered another stray, a marine who visited me from the farthest reaches of Long Island, traveling from almost as far away as the Hamptons. The sex was not good (he himself kept saying that he was stricken with what he called "the Irish curse," meaning a small cock), but our conversation after sex was better than what I generally have with my conquests, and it helped clarify for me what these men are seeking from transsexuals and drag queens. He told me that he had had his first experience with a transvestite when on duty in Southeast Asia where one night he met in a bar a gorgeous Indonesian woman, tall and slender, who took him back to her apartment. He insisted, as they all do, that he "had no idea" she was a man and described one of those classic "Crying Game" coups de théâtre where the robe is flung open only to reveal a throbbing erection (always enormous) where he had expected something less . . . protuberant. Again and again, men describe to me the same scene, a moment of brilliant theater, a spectacular unmasking, an epiphany of sorts that shocks them into arousal. This flabbergasting disclosure disarms all of their prejudices and leaves them speechless, paralyzed, unable to do anything but stare. Incomprehension has much the same effect on their sexual responses as actual physical bondage. Men who are tied to their bedposts are not responsible for their actions, and likewise men whose powers of reason have been knocked out by a bolt from the blue like a transformer by lightning cannot be held accountable for their short-lived experiments with homosexuality. After all, they were caught off-guard and moreover were led into the experience unwittingly, ensnared in a web of intrigue, the plot of a dishonest temptress who fooled them with her bewitching disguise. I would hazard a guess, and it is only a guess, that most men who describe to me their consternation at finding themselves within inches of something they've spent their whole life avoiding are being disingenuous, that they indeed had their little suspicions about "Lola" all along, and that her innocent "victim" doth protest too much, claiming to have been taken unawares when in fact he was primed for the experience.

If they were indeed genuinely surprised, what must they have seen when the "surprise" emerged? Perhaps their first thought was that they were looking at monstrous female genitalia, swollen labia and a gigantic clitoris which, rather than disgusting them as a genetic anomaly, turned them on, suggesting that Lola was experiencing an abnormal degree of arousal. Indeed, it is common practice among men attracted to transsexuals to refer to their partner's penis as a clitoris, a "big clitty," an expression that is perhaps a concession to the she-male's sensitivity about her gender and her attempt to efface it with everything from collagen injections to nomenclature.

It would be a very gullible man indeed who mistook an erect penis for a clitoris but perhaps in that instant of incomprehension, before they can make sense of what they are seeing, before it assumes a recognizable form, they identify it with a clitoris and perhaps this fusion leaves a lasting impression, allowing them to perceive the penis *through* the clitoris, as a distended organ, and therefore as something much less threatening and unfamiliar than a cock. What's more, the cock is almost always described with the exact same words: not just as an erection but as an erection "bulging out of a pair of panties," as if it belonged there and had not been grafted onto the crotch in the same way that the surrealist sculptor Hans Bellmer once grafted acrylic breasts onto his dolls' knees and legs to their shoulders. Men frequently describe the transsexual's penis not as an object in itself, but as an object within satin underwear, an image that suggests that the woman who wears the satin panties and the man who desires them have become one and the same person, that the sexes have fused, achieved platonic unity in the heat of lust.

The conceit of the besatined penis is also the ultimate oxymoron, the ultimate conjunction of opposites, of the sweet and the sour, the attractive and the repulsive, a mixture that creates something more than simple, uncomplicated desire but a feeling of excitement seething with paradox and irresolution. In this incongruity, one sees the essence of the whole drag aesthetic, which never provokes unqualified desire but a response full of contradictions. When these contradictions are fused into a single body, the viewer is thrown into a state of erotic confusion, forced to stare at the androgyne in order to get his bearings, to put his reactions in order, pigeonhole them according to the aesthetic that has heretofore governed his entire world—namely, female good, male bad.

Perhaps men are also attracted to drag queens because they feel privy to a secret, part of a conspiracy whose surreptitiousness heightens desire by creating a sense of menaced exclusivity. The more discretion either party must exercise, the more exciting the misbehavior, which occurs indoors, free of witnesses but constantly endangered by exposure, a threat that makes these furtive couplings all the more stealthy and unauthorized. An age of sexual openness like our own is nostalgic for a time of recreational culpability. The drag queen's secret—the surprise she is hiding beneath her satin panties—heightens feelings of criminal complicity between sexual outlaws, an aphrodisiac for a society in which candor is winning out over the pleasures of the impermissible.

Her

My satin panties conceal a surprise less astonishing than that concealed by my wigs—namely, my baldness. Last night I dreamt that I saw three separate women who live in my building wearing the same wig that I've worn for the last three months, the "new and truly unique" "daring fashion statement" named Maggie. My first thought was "Oh God, do I look as bad in Maggie as they do?" and then took some comfort in the thought that Maggie was clearly a rip-off, that she herself was at fault, and that some small part of my own ugliness can be attributed to the tendency of her luxurious, bouncing curls, which glistened with such healthy luster in Wigsalon.com's advertisement, to disintegrate into a dry bramble fixed on the top of one's head like a withered shrub. I remember seeing one woman in the elevator, a homely, obviously depressed person who rested what remained of Maggie's wanton tresses against the wall, her back to the door, as if she too were ashamed of her ugliness and sought to hide it from me by averting her face. It was all I could do to keep from reaching out and touching her frizzy hair, and saying, "I wear the same wig," but I stopped when it suddenly occurred to me that women do not want their wigs to be spotted and that my comment would be received, not as a mere statement of surprise about a coincidence, but as an insult.

What does it mean, Dr. Freud? For one, it reflects my anxiety about the new wig purchases I've been making, all of them expensive

mistakes made in an effort to find the elusive cure, the perfect costume, the Holy Grail that will magically rejuvenate and feminize my
haggard male face. But my dream also suggests that I could not legitimately make that gesture of solidarity with another wig wearer
because no one wants to join an ugliness club, however consoling it is
to find others in the same predicament, other victims of the practical
jokes of the vicious hag Maggie. Nor would it be any too pleasant for a
woman to think that an accessory pivotal to her appearance is also
worn by a figure as tasteless as a drag queen. Women usually do
not wear wigs with the same freedom as cross-dressers do, donning
them at their convenience, but use them to cover up disfiguring ail-
ments, a hereditary predisposition toward thinning hair, the baldness
caused by chemotherapy, or simply an unmanageable head of split
ends. Only very chic women wear wigs for fun, and then the wigs they
choose are rarely "passable," but clearly synthetic, unnaturally
straight, or even dyed zany clown colors. The facetiousness with
which they show off the stylish artificiality of their coiffures is more
akin to my own motives for wearing Maggie and Karen, reflecting a
license that most wig wearers do not have, the license to go bare-
headed, to remove whenever we choose what is to others a type of
bandage. When I reached out to touch the poor plain Jane in the elevator, I did so as someone from an altogether-different world,
someone whose wig is a fashion accessory, and thus could not legitimately claim solidarity with other martyrs of Maggie's false promises.

I will never be a true sister to a straight woman, and yet in the last
year I have gotten closer to women than I have ever been before. I
even find myself wondering if my newfound appreciation for feminine self-presentation could ever be eroticized. Could my attentive-
ness ever mutate, shifting just a few centimeters to the left, into a
decidedly lesbian desire to possess what I admire? Recently my
cleaning lady Brenda showed me photographs of her family, and I
found myself passing over the pictures of her handsome son and fix-
ating instead on her gorgeous daughter whose makeup, I could not
stop repeating, much to Brenda's bewilderment, was perfect. Again

and again, she proffered photographs of her slighted son, as if to say, "Pay attention to him too," but I had eyes only for the daughter whose appearance I was now busily dismantling into its various cosmetic components. When, if ever, does looking and admiring become desiring? As a gay man, I certainly wasn't indifferent to the appearance of women, but, a gullible victim of general impressions, I never looked closely, never had a reason to puzzle out the mysteries of a well-tweezered brow or a flattering shade of eye shadow. I have always considered myself a stubborn six on the Kinsey scale, but now, at the very moment I am at my most feminine, I find myself thrust into an unprecedentedly intimate relation with the opposite sex, an intimacy in which my desire to look like a woman and my exhilaration at having become an initiate into the lore of "beauty secrets" has removed a barrier between me and a gender I have deliberately chosen not to desire. I am closer to being a straight man as a woman than as a homosexual male. The effacement of my gender has paradoxically led to its backhanded affirmation, to an unexpected awakening of heterosexual interest and curiosity about the bodies of a sex I have made a concerted policy of ignoring. And herein lies an explanation of the straight man's gruff indifference to the bodies of other men, an indifference that not infrequently turns into hostility when by accident men are forced into close proximity to each other and must take notice of the appearance of their rivals. The heterosexual male's refusal to look, his policy of averting his eyes, is a prophylactic measure that forestalls desire, ensuring that he remains in a state of ignorance, that his curiosity is never awakened. To know the male body is to love it, and so to prevent the unconscionable from happening, one must simply never allow one's eyes to focus on another man's anatomy. Surely this is one of the reasons it is easier for women to have lesbian experiences than straight men to have gay ones, since women *do* look at each other, and therefore place themselves in a state that, however innocent, is always a prelude to desire, the state of curiosity.

Him

It is hard to avoid looking at the male anatomy in prison. A man I met online confessed to me the other day that he had spent a good chunk of his youth on Rikers Island, where he served a sentence for dealing drugs and committing unspecified crimes that he boasted made him "more interesting than a book." He described himself as a large black man, over 6'3'' and weighing 245 pounds, who needed to find a "little buddy" in order to satisfy the need alluded to in his screen name, "NYCButtwatcher." He told me that he had long ago gotten his life together and now owned a home with his wife, where they lived happily with their two young children, although he still couldn't get Rikers completely out of his system, having acquired in prison a taste for pederasty that remains with him long after his release. Unlike most men I speak to online, he referred to me unabashedly as a man and did not pretend that I was a "beautiful lady." In fact, he made a rather feeble joke at one point that he both lives in Queens and loves queens, a bon mot that suggests that he is quite conscious of wanting to have sex with a man, however effeminate, a preference that smacks of furtive jailhouse intimacies.

Prison creates for most men a set of circumstances similar to those that drag has created for me: the inability to avert one's eyes from a sex one seldom notices, let alone desires. It is not just that prisoners are making do in the absence of women, that they are opportunists, that they use rape to manipulate others into positions of subordination within the hierarchy of power that prevails in such harsh settings, as their temporary diversions into homosexuality are usually explained. Their experiments with men are indeed all of these things, but they represent something more as well: the discovery of a new aesthetic, the sudden awakening to the appearance of their own gender. The prevalence of men means that the eye has nowhere to turn, and because we inevitably seek out the human form in our immediate surroundings, the eyes of prisoners by default alight with a new degree of attention and curiosity on their fellow inmates, much as my eyes have alighted on the opposite sex now that I am striving to mimic their makeup and mannerisms. I return to my admittedly unscientific conviction that cops and firemen are particularly infatuated with drag queens because proximity—indeed, the complete dependence of those working in such professions on their colleagues for safety—makes it impossible to ignore one's own sex. But if this were really the case, wouldn't sports figures also be drag-queen admirers, which, to my knowledge, they are not? According to this theory, physicians and portrait painters should also be functioning bisexuals since they, too, make their livings by exercising intimate knowledge of the male physique.

The day before yesterday, I met another man, this one only twenty-two, who said that he had spent part of his youth in a reformatory and was presently on probation, carefully monitored by some sort of "home escort" or electronic-surveillance system, his punishment for dealing crack, which he told me in passing he had sold since the tender age of twelve. This was a surprising and not-altogether-welcome revelation, coming as it did during pillow talk. At one point, he bolted upright and asked me the time, anxious lest he miss his mandatory 7:00 appointment, one of two he was required to keep every day as part of a plea bargain that kept him out of an upstate penitentiary. "Crack dealer" is the last thing one would think of, looking into those angelic eyes, and I suddenly felt alarmed at my recklessness in inviting him over and began wondering if, in my depression, my hopelessness, I have not let down my guard and am courting danger, like every other aging gay john I thought I would never become. These feelings were confirmed today when he called me late in the evening to ask me if he could have a small loan to tide him over until payday.

Following hard on the heels of my encounter with my Rikers Island admirer, the incident made me ask myself where this project is leading me: to a book contract or to a slab in the county morgue (in which case I pity the poor bewildered coroner)? I have never been attracted to rough trade, and yet rough trade comes with the territory of cross-dressing, perhaps because of past prison experiences and perhaps because the criminal element is a sexually retrograde lot, sadly out of step with the androgynous look and behavior of the modern woman.

In a crack between my mattress and the wood platform of my bed, I hide a small canister of Mace, a present from my mother who gave it to me with her blessings and her sincere hope that I would never need to use it on any of my tricks. I am thus literally sleeping with a weapon in my bed, much as some people sleep with guns beneath their pillows. In the back of my mind is a horrific incident that occurred in Boston in the 1980s to a friend of a friend, a miserable alcoholic who could not keep his paws off lower-class straight boys, one of whom broke into his apartment with a friend and murdered him, presumably because he refused to hand over the keys to his car. He did not go down without a struggle, but fought back so fiercely that the entire apartment was destroyed and he was found in the bathroom amidst the wreckage of the broken sink and commode, his head nearly severed from his body. I think of his murder now that my life has become a parade of strangers, now that I have settled into the seemingly unbreakable habit of depression, now that my own value and that of my work has fallen so precipitately that I do not care what happens to me. My despondence makes me imprudent and therefore places me in harm's way, a danger that I mistake for pleasure, a pleasure I need to alleviate the misery I feel.

I am amazed by how unprecious my life has become. And yet depression is proving rather useful to me at the moment. Would I have been able to undertake this project—indeed, even conceive of it—if I weren't so stubbornly depressed? Depression has made me fearless, so unattached to life that I respect nothing, feel obligated to no one, am indifferent to public opinion, which cannot reach me in this distant land that I have entered, far, far away on the farthest shores of ennui. One assumes that courage emanates from strength, from a feeling of indomitability, but it can also emanate from weakness, from an all-consuming sense of the unimportance of things, from a desperate lack of appetite for life. I am fearless as old people are fearless, doddering crones and addled dotards with so little to lose that they find themselves buoyed up by a sense of their sheer expendability, becoming more reckless the more transparent they feel, able to pull the wool over society's eyes with impunity because they know that no one is looking, no one is keeping track of them, no one cares. Those chattering voices in my head, telling me not to embarrass myself, cautioning me to look before I leap, lecturing me that others will see me, judge me, ostracize me, have been quieted by the pervasive hopelessness that has settled over me like the proverbial bell jar, blocking out all noise, all sounds of distant disapproval.

I have discussed how drag came to my rescue at the very minute my powers to captivate were slipping, and yet it is not a miracle cure for menopause and in some respects has even made me older than my years. Never before has there been such a discrepancy in age between me and my partners, virtually all of whom I rob from the online cradle. Drag has put me in the undignified position of the typical middle-aged john preying on young tricks, boys in their late teens who, since the balance of desire between us is so unequal, so weighted in their favor, frequently attempt to narrow the gulf that divides us by asking for five-dollar loans. Dressing in women's clothing has paradoxically made me a more conventional gay man, in the sense that it has ushered into my love life something I never believed I was capable of falling for: namely, trade, the young stripling proles who are so attracted to the aesthetic of drag. Denial was intended to buy me a reprieve from old age, but her taste in teenagers has left me with one stiletto planted firmly in the grave.

Her

Conventional gay men, however, do not usually guard their closet doors with the same degree of vigilance that I exercise. I have betrayed my high principles and tried to conceal my drag activities. Since I'm working more at the law firm, I decided to hire a cleaning lady for the first time in my life, and was fortunate enough to find Brenda, an astonishingly meticulous Polish woman who might as well be employed by a forensics lab, so thoroughly does she dust every object in my rooms, crawling around on her hands and knees picking up buttons, pennies, and chewed-up pen caps. She finds other things as well: empty condom wrappers, the backs of earrings, beads from broken necklaces, my eyeliner brush, a barrette, an empty tube of K-Y, and a false eyelash. After she cleaned my freezer, I found the four bottles of poppers I store there arranged in a neat row. Yesterday after she left, I spotted a single fake plastic nail sitting on a coaster by my recliner where she had obviously placed it. I try to imagine what she must have thought when she found it on the floor, the instant of discovery, the moment she asked herself what this strange object was, if she should throw it out or keep it, and then the gesture she made as she placed it on the coaster, a slow, thoughtful movement, which, as I recreate it in my mind's eye, seems almost Jamesian in its indecisiveness, full of a puzzled hesitation that signaled a dawning awareness, a dim perception, a realization taking form. How long will it be before it occurs to her that I am a drag queen? How many bobby pins and hair clips does she need to pick up before she knows for sure that there is no mysterious female occupant holed up somewhere in my apartment, no "secret sharer"? Will there be a moment of truth? Will she whip open the door of the closet in my bedroom that I always keep closed because it contains my wigs and costumes, and shriek as one of the Styrofoam heads bearing Maggie or Karen comes tumbling out into her arms, shaking and tossing like something angry and alive? Will she stare in dismay at the dozens of minidresses and fishnet teddies and imagine me tiptoeing up behind her and striking her down like one of the transvestite assassins in Hollywood slasher films, monsters whose perversions lead them to slaughter innocent women to the accompaniment of scores as loud and ghastly as car alarms? Or will the realization sneak up on her almost imperceptibly, unconsciously, until one day she simply knows what I am? Will the expression on her face change when she talks to me and will she lower her eyes in embarrassment? Or will she even care or, better still, be amused, having seen *La Cage aux Folles, Tootsie,* and *Hairspray* and been touched by the laughable antics of hideous buffoons so helpless and feminine that even she—an abnormally helpless and shy woman herself—can condescend to them?

Every time she comes, I put away my costumes and makeup, guiltily effacing all of Denial's traces, stuffing her back in the bedroom closet. It is not as if I am afraid that Brenda will find out or if I really even care to an inordinate degree, but she is such a good maid and, what's more, such a sweet woman that I would hate to alienate her, or at least this is what I tell myself. Perhaps I lock Denial up because I am ashamed of her, like the madwoman in the attic, afraid that she will slip past her keeper and set the house ablaze while everyone is sleeping. When the maid is here, I am acutely aware of the apartment's other occupant who is always just out of sight, always in danger of being spotted, the train of her dress slipping around a corner as she flees, an abandoned cigarette left smoking in an ashtray as she dashes into the other room, a tissue bearing the scarlet impression of two lips dropped in haste on the floor as the broom sweeps ever nearer.

This morning, I experienced the same fear of exposure in the presence of the dour Indian doctor who gave me my annual physical. How my heart sank when I entered her office (this was my first appointment with her) and saw her sitting there humorlessly, to all appearances catatonic, not a flicker of a smile passing across her face, nor even the most perfunctory of acknowledgments issuing from her lips. I must admit that I am prejudiced against Indian doctors, a feeling that goes all the way back to summer school in the late 1970s, when I had a few unfortunate encounters with a homophobe from Calcutta at the Harvard student clinic where my requests for various venereal tests, particularly for anal gonorrhea, were met with disgusted disbelief and once with a lecture about the medical threat that I, an STD-ridden pariah, posed to my society (a libelous accusation since I can say in all honesty that I have never once tested positive for a venereal disease, from HIV to syphilis to chlamydia).

I never feel more urgently the need for gay liberationists than when I am in a doctor's office, where the Hippocratic oath seems to fly out the window, leaving me at the mercy of someone who despises me and who, if they weren't constrained by ethical considerations and, let us hope, by the dispassion of science, could very easily hurt me. She ushered me over to the examination table where it suddenly occurred to me that I would have to remove my clothing and that she could scarcely keep from noticing that my entire body, from my forearms to my toes, was shaven, a fact that could lead her to only one conclusion and me to one fate: death by prescription pad at the hands of this Hindu Lucrezia Borgia. Mercifully, the cost-savings measures of HMOs came to my rescue and my annual physical consisted solely of her rolling up my sleeve and taking my blood pressure, which only goes to prove that one doesn't necessarily have to be gay (she in all probability hadn't guessed from the sentence or two I had uttered) to be killed by the health system.

Once again, the terrorist in a teddy proves to be bourgeois at heart. On the one hand, I can hang myself up as a piñata in various chat rooms and parry the blows leveled at me, but on the other, I am timid as a mouse in the face of someone as harmless as my cleaning lady or a doctor. My courage is highly selective and contextual. When I am working at the law firm, I pass around among my colleagues the photographs I take of myself in drag, whereas when I am at home, I cower behind my door when I must open it to welcome my visitors. In one sharply divided personality, I combine outrageous heedlessness of public opinion with anguished servility to it.

This servility reached its limit last Friday. On the day of Michael Jackson's arrest for child molestation, a woman who lives in my building and with whom I've been friendly for two and a half years told me that I ask her children too many questions and that she doesn't want me to talk to them any more. I was naturally dismayed and so hurt that all I could say was "I'm terribly sorry," quickly disengaging from the encounter so that I could run back to my apartment, where I took solace in the bottle, sobbing while I drank. What astonished me most about the incident is that she has always greeted me so warmly in passing and even smiled sweetly as I chatted with her children, seemingly indifferent to such insidious questions as "Where do you go to school?" "Do you like school?" and "What grade are you in?"—an interrogation that she apparently interpreted as a molester's fact-finding mission, an attempt to pry out of her precious darlings their exact whereabouts so that I could swoop down on the playground as they dangled from the jungle gym and carry them off to my torture chamber to slake my perverted lusts. Every time she saw me coming she must have thought to herself, "Here comes the big pervert, I'd better be friendly in order to appease him so he won't capture my kids and then sell them off on the black market to the neighborhood kiddie-porn ring or to pederastic sheiks in Saudi Arabia." My intuition, usually uncannily accurate in assessing people's facial expressions, failed me entirely here, and I interpreted her growing alarm as neighborly goodwill.

I write about this horrific encounter not only because it upset me deeply, but because it has temporarily intensified the pariah complex I developed since I moved to this largely black neighborhood where ill-behaved children, who pose a far greater threat to me than I do to them, taunt me to my face and comment obscenely about my girlish ass and its inimitable swish. Never in any of the many places I have lived have I felt more acutely the presence of homophobia, which naturally I have experienced before, but only on rare occasions—so rare in fact that its threat has become largely theoretical, an abstract menace that, after decades of relative complacency, I am in some respects unprepared to face. And at the very moment that I purchase an apartment in a morally righteous community, a lower-middle-class neighborhood anxious to keep its streets free of the criminal element (and the distinction it makes between hoodlums and godless reprobates like myself is none too fine), I choose to transgress the ultimate taboo and ensnare its menfolk in my unspeakably naughty wiles.

I am dumbfounded by my neighbor's provinciality. Unacquainted with homosexuals, even though she lives in a city with one of the largest gay populations in the world, she equates them with pedophiles, making an illogical connection between a single gay man, large and effeminate, and a nefarious child predator. If she only knew the whole truth about the shenanigans of Denial, she would gather her children in her arms and run screaming for the hills, stopping only to activate the Amber Alert system. When I told my friends at the law firm about our encounter, we spent the day making jokes about my perverted proclivities, deciding that the best way to handle the predicament is to drop by her apartment in full drag and volunteer to baby-sit, proffering handfuls of lollipops and pocketsful of Gummi Bears.

I am forty-six, I am entirely alone, I am a drag queen, I have no profession, and the last thing I need to perfect my alienation is to begin scaring kids, whose jittery parents view me as a monster, looking at me askance in the elevator as if to say, "Get thee behind me, Satan." In another age, I might have been hunted as a witch, burned at the stake for desecrating the host and cavorting on the altar astride a billy goat. As Denial, I desecrate the mores of an evangelical minority not known for its tolerance of sexual dissidents, eliciting the social disapproval that actually gives me the courage to continue. One has to hold one's society in a high degree of contempt to invert the sacred categories of man and woman, especially in a community in which men are frequently accused of shirking their manly duties and women of wearing the pants by default. There is a sense in which the black community is already in drag, the women having assumed the role of paterfamilias in the face of decades of deadbeat dads, a sociological phenomenon that perhaps explains their intolerance of homosexuality, exhausted as they are by the chronic inversion of sexual roles that has plagued their families since slave owners systematically split them apart.

I am sickened by the Michael Jackson affair. It is difficult to imagine a less-appealing person, and yet the savagery of the press and the bloodlust of the public make me rally to his cause, pooh-poohing his misdemeanors, which, if he is indeed guilty of child molestation, probably consisted of nothing more brutal than petting and cuddling. The mother making the accusations is clearly a gold digger, for what parent in her right mind would pack her child off to Neverland if she weren't dangling little Timmy or little Joey before Jackson's nose as live bait, the dollar signs ringing up in her eyes with every pinch on the cheek and pat on the tail?

Michael Jackson's cosmetic surgeon may just as well have been an artist in a Hollywood special-effects studio. His patient's features are more macabre than the facial prosthetics actors wear in horror films, and perhaps because I too have created for recreational purposes my own type of prosthetic, I am unusually sensitive to the ill-treatment of other prosthesis wearers. The media is engaging in a good old-fashioned lynching, undoubtedly prehistoric in practice, the extermination of a deformed member of the tribe, a creature whose disfigurements it interprets as the mark of a malevolent god, the visible manifestations of his corrupt soul and contagious wickedness. As Denial, I, too, venture out into cyberspace as a tribal outcast, my face bearing the mark of Cain. Perhaps I feel a degree of esprit de corps with Michael as another grotesque, another monster stoned in the public square—although, unlike Michael, I pick up the stones and hurl them back at my persecutors and some of these projectiles, I am delighted to say, strike their targets with a satisfying thud.

Him

If, that is, they don't boomerang. Yesterday afternoon, during cocktail hour, my three-drink late-afternoon orgy, when I do all of my cruising, and most of my fucking, I received a phone call from a woman who seemed to have dialed the wrong number. A loud brassy voice with a heavy New York City accent asked, "Is this the service?" "The service?" I repeated, puzzled, and she replied nervously, "The service, the service . . . uh . . . the service for the doctor's office." I told her she had the wrong number, and she apologized and hung up. Only afterward did I realize what had happened. She had clearly been going through her husband's wallet and had found a piece of paper with my phone number and the word "service" written on it, a mystifying clue which she apparently thought referred to an escort agency, but which, in fact, referred to the "oral service" that, in my sex ads, I so anachronistically advertise as providing. I can only hope for her husband's sake that my voice and the bewilderment it expressed threw her off track and that she lost the scent of her wayward spouse's adulterous trail.

I find it strange and ridiculous to think that I, of all people, am finally the "other woman," the cause of jealousy, the mysterious dark lady behind the phone numbers that men slip into their wallets for safekeeping. I try to imagine the fear that must have driven this woman to call me, but I can't seem to summon up enough empathy to picture her anxiety, knowing full well that I posed no threat to her marriage whatsoever and may even have diverted extracurricular impulses far more hazardous to her relationship than a ten-minute blow job. I contrast my own relative indifference toward sex, an act as unimportant to me as taking a shower, with this woman's anger and paranoia about what she views as, to use an expression that captures my incomprehension at her old-fashioned fears, her husband's "two-timing." When I consider my own offhandedness in regard to sex, I realize how male I really am, how my carefree promiscuity is based on a typically masculine form of emotional disengagement, the cold-blooded dispassion of a man who has heartlessly severed fucking from affection. My caller's desperation reminds me that I am not the Other Woman at all, I am the Other Man. The very way in which I play girl makes me more boy. I am male not only by virtue of my bone structure, my titlessness, my five-o'clock shadow, my bass voice, and my Y chromosomes but by virtue of my voracious appetite for sex and my utter heedlessness of the consequences of the almighty Orgasm. Something besides the "little extra," the "surprise," the "bonus," makes sex with drag queens a homosexual act, namely, the uncanny reciprocity of desire between both parties whose relations exude fraternal like-mindedness.

Little did my caller know that, far from threatening my tricks' relationships, I do my part to shore them up, acting as an unlikely marriage counselor of sorts who, decked out in black lace, ministers to buck-naked patients who complain about their wives' acquisitiveness, frigidity, shrewishness, jealousy, and whininess. In my role as high Solomonic priestess of the pillow, I encourage them to exercise compassion, avoid unnecessary bickering, indulge in shameless flattery, and treat their lovers with the same measure of sensitivity with which I myself want to be treated by men, a lesson I have learned perched like a stylite atop these towering heels where I command a panoramic, bird's-eye view on relations between the sexes. Oddly enough, after I pester my tricks with questions, they frequently wax sentimental, begin praising their spouses to the skies, and then, inevitably, retrieve their wallets from their cast-off pants and show me their family photographs, not only of their wives but of their children, one of whom just got her first bike, another just started Little League, and still another joined the Brownies. Once I had a long conversation after sex with a man waffling over whether to ask his girlfriend to marry him, a decision so protracted that she was threatening to call it quits if he wouldn't stop dithering and take the plunge. I pressed him to describe her to me and, after he sang her praises, assumed the role of her advocate and pleaded her case, with the result that he left my apartment determined to return to her arms and pop the question that very evening. Assuming this wasn't all bluster (and certainly his eyes were full of stars when I led him to the door), some lucky newlywed owes her good fortune to an aging drag queen in Brooklyn who, sprawling sated in a fishnet teddy and a frizzy wig, somewhat disarranged after a long, hard, sweaty screw, convinced her husband that the time had come to tie the knot.

I inspire men with my literary talents as well. The other evening someone who professed deep respect for my work contacted me saying that we had met before, although I did not recognize his photograph. I asked for clarification, and he explained that he had met me as a man when I lived in Park Slope and that he had guessed who I was, obviously not on the basis of my drag photographs, but solely on the basis of the books listed in the bio I have posted on my Web site, titles he distinctly remembered seeing on my shelves. He then described one of the oddest evenings of my life, an adventure involving June, my former downstairs neighbor, a manic-depressive prostitute whose mad exploits really deserve a book in themselves.

One night I returned home around 11:00 P.M. after an exhausting twelve-hour shift at the law firm only to be greeted at my door by June and a companion, a plump man in his thirties who stood in the hallway in a pair of graying underpants. Surprised but not dismayed, since I never underestimated June's capacity to astonish, I invited them in, offered them drinks, and waited while she explained that her trick, whom, to my dismay, she promptly walloped across the face, had just cleaned her apartment. Now that they had finished with hers, she fully intended for him to clean mine, which at the moment was so filthy that it didn't need to be cleaned so much as hosed out like the Augean stable. I could not look a gift horse in the mouth, and so I agreed, but I first took the boy aside and asked him if he really wanted to clean my apartment and if he were sure he was having a good time, a gesture that he remembered years later when he contacted me. I then went down-stairs to June's cradling my vodka bottle and used her computer to cruise for two hours while they dusted and mopped above me, with June screeching commands like a lieutenant in the Gestapo, and every now and then delivering a resounding whack to his thinly clad buttocks. He remembered the titles of my books because, in a gesture expressive of her love for me, she had made him dust them and then, dissatisfied with his job, had reddened his already-well-paddled bottom and insisted that he do it all over again.

When we spoke online, he told me that he hadn't really enjoyed the evening after all, that June made a very hammy dominatrix, and when I questioned him, saying that I thought dominatrices were by definition hammy, he told me that he preferred a much more subdued, naturalistic performance and that simply being ignored while he cleaned was enough of an affront to his dignity to arouse him. After they finished with my apartment (a lousy job, I might add), they returned to June's where she made the strategic mistake of taking him to bed in a thoughtful attempt to repay him for his housecleaning services, an entirely unnecessary move, he said, and one that made him feel even less abused since what he really wanted was to be disregarded, taken for granted, exploited, and sent packing. He told me that "her pussy was old," whatever that means (certainly it got a lot of use), that he thought she was wearing false teeth (in fact, her teeth are all rotten and capped), that her breath smelled overpoweringly of bubble gum (her mouth is a charnel house without it), and that her enormous breasts were two concrete cones that cantilevered out from her chest defying gravity (the result of her ample implants or, as she called them, her "augmentations"). I felt a rush of pity for my old friend when he told me this. June is my age—forty-six—has never learned any skill other than fucking, and now that she is getting old, although by most standards she still looks magnificent (even if she is something of a Frankenstein after all of her nose jobs, face-lifts, and cheek and boob implants), she has become an entirely superfluous human being, little more than a glory hole into which men stick their cocks and ejaculate. To think of her there with her leathery, overused pussy and bubble-gum breath, trying her best to bring pleasure to a man whose libido was too complex for her to understand, breaks my heart and brings back memories of the friendship I abandoned, disturbed as I was by the chaotic effect on my life of her drinking, drug taking, and emotional volatility.

After my masochist identified himself and reminded me of this episode, he and I began spontaneously to open our hearts to each other. He told me how much he admired me for my literary accomplishments (which of course he'd only dusted, not read) and I, in turn, as is my griping, disenchanted wont, vigorously pooh-poohed them, lamenting my failure as a writer, my sad love affairs, my tragic social life, my extreme loneliness, my habitual despondence—the customary litany of grievances which, after years of practice, I am unusually adept at summoning forth in convincingly plaintive and self-pitying detail. He in turn began to pour out his own sorrows, telling a haunting tale of the frustration of his ambitions, the foundering of his promising youth as the valedictorian of one of New York's most exclusive prep schools, and his present lonely existence, destitute, still living at home at the age of thirty-three with a catatonic father he nonetheless adores. He now works as a substitute grade-school teacher and told me that every day he feels his brain atrophying from disuse, the range of his thoughts shrinking to one dry patch of dull, monotonous routine. My heart immediately went out to him since I know this terrible sense of intellectual diminishment all too well, feel my own mind following ever-narrower paths of habit, unable to think the thoughts I once flattered myself I would always be able to think. I have reached a time in my life when I have begun to mourn the waste of my unchallenged, untested, unexercised mind, now flabby and complacent, a regret as keen, as tangible, as the grief I feel watching the slow dilapidation of my body as I slide into middle age.

If the Internet is a fallow field for lies, as my own charades suggest, it is also a fallow field for truths, for naked confessions, for reckless revelations that one would be reluctant to make to a friend but that one makes with injudicious candor to a perfect stranger. Why is it so easy to be intimate with those we will never meet? Why do our cyber playmates provide the perfect ear in which to whisper dreaded confidences? Entrusting our secrets to these electronic house guests, who appear on our keyboards and then, with a single keystroke, vanish, would appear to be a sordid indiscretion, the potentially wounding gossip of a compulsive tattletale who makes chitchat out of his own tragedies. And yet in most regards, there is no safer repository of secrets than a stranger. Because we do not know him—most likely never will—he cannot use against us the damning information we supply him, unlike our most intimate friends, who could indeed find a use for our confessions should there be an unintended betrayal, a sudden shift in alliances, or even an irreparable break. The Internet is as tempting a place to spill one's guts as the pillow is after sex. One is not liberating one's skeletons from their closet, one is simply taking them out for a waltz around the room, granting them a highly supervised furlough from the dungeon in which we confine them. Bones will rattle no matter how dark the closet, and it is this constant clatter echoing in our conscience that makes us long to throw open the door and let them out, even if they are released into a holding pen as discreet and anonymous as the Internet.

Her

C losets, however, are preferable, it would seem, to chat rooms. There's been another episode in my ongoing quarrel with Bronxcenterfold who keeps changing her screen name, I flatter myself for the purpose of avoiding my wrath. On New Year's Eve, as I waited for an eighteen-year-old black virgin to drop by for his deflowering, I entered the NYCShemale4males chat room where a girl by the name of Delvar7 was attacking a rather pretty drag queen, who, although she looked good in her photos, was slightly broad in the beam. Delvar7 began calling her piggy, piglet, porky, sow, and hog and simply wouldn't let up, at one point even calling out "sueeeyyy." I recognized something familiar about her imaginative misspellings and asked if she were Bronxcenterfold. She admitted it readily, and so I mounted my highest horse and entered the fray, defending the drag queen with a vehemence that perhaps she didn't really appreciate, since the implication was that she needed defending, that she was as ugly as her detractor made her out to be.

Bronx and I tore into each other for a few minutes, pulling hair and blackening eyes, until I decided to return to my old trick of quotation and sent to every member of the room the description I wrote of my last encounter with this harpy, a passage that itself quoted a report of a previous skirmish. After I spammed them, a moment of guilty silence fell upon the room and girls too cowardly to speak out in my favor, at least in front of others, contacted me privately to tell me not to let her get under my skin, that "what comes around goes around," and that—how consoling—"you are as beautiful as you feel." One girl even asked me if I believed in "the Good Book" and, not wanting to discourage her when she was clearly trying to comfort me, I told her that I did, whereupon she advised me to place my trust in religion and have faith in "the dear baby Jesus," who, in his infinite wisdom and compassion for All God's Creatures, would "fry that bitch" for her sins.

I wish I could say that I had taught my sisters a lesson in brotherly love and persuaded them to search their consciences about their mistreatment of others, but the truth is that I have simply browbeaten them into accepting me by delivering an ultimatum: Insult me and feel the heat, call me ugly and suffer the consequences of my fleet fingers. They have learned the hard way that Ms. Desire has a foul temper and an even sharper tongue and that cutting comments about her by-now-infamous appearance will unleash a flood of scurrilous remarks typed at speeds her employers have clocked at 100 words per minute. Moreover, one false move and you are trapped forever, like a fly in amber, in the pages of her book, which she is known to quote to potential customers, who agree wholeheartedly with her statements about your spitefulness and unfeminine ferocity.

I have also won their begrudging tolerance through a Machiavellian campaign of ingratiating myself to them with flattery. Like all of the girls, I frequently check out the photographs of the other contenders in the room and, provided that they aren't out-and-out Quasimodos, which they are at least 50 percent of the time, am very generous with my compliments, zeroing in on the one marginally feminine feature in an otherwise-unpassable face. Naturally, I hope to reap future dividends of moral support when I am being ripped limb from limb by the angry mob, a hope dashed every time I am cornered, but it is also true that I feel that the girls need flattery, are starved for it, that they are as insecure as I am, and that the only humane thing to do is stretch the truth and tell that fat androgyne from Hoboken bulging out of her latex dominatrix outfit and that wizened Cambodian with the jagged scar slashed across her cheek that they are goddesses.

I have also been known to refrain from exploiting to my advantage their ugliness when the gloves come off. The other day I was exchanging pleasantries with a girl I did not know when she began quite spontaneously, without provocation, to insult me, asking me why *ever* I had decided to put on a dress and if my boots and spandex mini were an appropriate outfit for my job on the oil rig. Startled by her hostility, I immediately checked her photograph, only to discover, to my amazement, that, far from being even marginally passable, she was a fat, frowsy transsexual in a wrinkled muumuu, absolutely the last creature to risk taking me to task for my homeliness and manly physique. It would have been easy to tell the pot to desist or the kettle would grab the scouring pad and scratch off her Teflon coating, but I refrained—not because I felt I ought to play fair, but because I realized that she had so much more vested in her appearance than I do and that my heaviest artillery would have been overkill in light of the situation.

I did ask her though why ever *she* had decided to put on a dress (I believe I said "that rag from the 50¢ bin of the Salvation Army") and she responded that the reason was quite simple: "*I* [as opposed to you] was born that way." The transsexuals I have met online often deny their gender by evoking myths of feminine souls trapped by an accident of reincarnation in masculine bodies, a myth of sexual samsara that explains in part the ambivalence if not outright contempt they feel toward homosexuals. Because they think of themselves as real women with a healthy attraction to the opposite sex, they seek to disassociate themselves from gay men, disparaging "fags" in order to buttress the all-too-assailable fantasy of their heterosexuality. Homophobia is thus a key part of their disguise, of the way they reclassify themselves, defecting from one gender to another, from gay men to women, arrogating to themselves a label they cannot legitimately claim but that they cling to through their constant protestations of disgust at the effeminate behavior of sissies and butch queens. They are obsessed with homosexuality and their chat-room chatter abounds with words like "fucking fagit," "queer," and "cocksucking fag," derisive epithets for men whose limp-wristed mannerisms are parodies of their own authentic femininity. By hating gay men, they set themselves apart from a minority whose perversions confirm the normality of their own desires as proper young ladies with conventional aspirations of becoming housewives to he-men who bring home the bacon and then collapse on the sofa to watch contact sports while their happily indentured servants prepare refreshments in the kitchen. In this way, one set of monsters exploits another set in order to make themselves seem less monstrous. Because I cannot stand to watch others deceive themselves, I admit as often as I can that I am a gay man and, what's more, that I am not alone, that, like it or not, all of the girls in the room are gay men, that we are all men in dresses, a proclamation especially unwelcome among boys who have gone so much further than I have in this masquerade, assuming costumes of flesh and blood, of progesterone and silicone gel.

Him

They are not the only ones deceiving themselves. The men who pursue them also tell little white lies. I am bored with the sex I have been having—indeed, I am occasionally revolted by it—and wonder if I can bear to see this project through to the bitter end if I have more encounters like the date I had the day before yesterday. I was cruising online when I was contacted by a gorgeous Puerto Rican who said that he wanted to have his first experience with a cross-dresser and that, since I was pretty—more to the point, since I was *free*—he had chosen *me* as the "lucky girl"! He was dark, muscular, and thrillingly masculine, and I was delighted by the prospect of taking him "to the other side." In the course of flirting with him, I asked if he would talk to me while we made love—nothing fancy, just the usual clichés of dirty talk which I have come to enjoy, not for their filthiness, but simply because I adore men's voices and am aroused by them during sex. Latin men in particular have been taught to croon an unctuous shtick in your ear as they make love and I find this auditory dimension of domination—even when plagiarized from the sound tracks of skin flicks—irresistible.

When he arrived, he was wearing a heavy overcoat that came down well past his knees and his face and neck were bundled up in a scarf, a wintry disguise that concealed from me a disturbing fact, that since the time his photograph was taken, some fifteen summers had passed and, during that time, many, many Taco Bell Baja Beef Gorditas and Chicken Fiesta Burritos had been consumed, leaving my stallion a pasty, potbellied tub of lard. I had just hung up his coat and was about to retrieve it and ask him to leave when he ordered me "down on my knees," the opening salvo of what was to be an hour of begrudgingly obeyed commands. Against my will, I felt my knees buckle and I sank to the floor before his protuberant belly as he opened his pants to reveal a penis no larger than a pacifier. I felt panicked to be in this position and cursed myself for giving in to the bullying of a bald-faced liar, whom I had stupidly failed to kick out of my apartment, not because I was reluctant to hurt his feelings, but because I was paralyzed with embarrassment, unable to say out loud, "You openly deceived me, you scoundrel," dismissing him with the vicious candor he fully deserved but that I did not have the courage to muster. And to make matters worse, I had passed the point of no return by sinking to my knees, thus losing the strategic advantage of standing in front of him face to face, a posture from which I could more easily have sent him on his way, an act of violent self-assertion difficult to perform under any circumstances but impossible while cowering in a fishnet teddy on one's living room-floor. Opportunists like this man may very well count on their prey experiencing this paralysis and succumbing to their unwelcome advances out of shame, out of taboos against insulting strangers, a courtesy that they themselves have failed to extend to us and but that we are forced to extend to them because we are bound by the ironclad obligations of politeness. Either they are straightforward con artists or, to take a more charitable view, they suffer from such a distorted view of their bodies that they have no conception that they have been guilty of fraud and present themselves to their tricks more or less as anorexics present themselves to their mirrors.

Leaping to my feet and screaming "Enough!" was out of the question given how difficult it is, not only to insult strangers but to rise and get my balance while wearing my stiletto boots, and so

I resolved to go through with the irksome routine, hoping that I could dispatch him quickly with an expertly administered blow job, but to no avail. He was in it for the long haul, was going to take his time and savor this novel experience, and—worse—he was going to narrate the whole sorry episode as I had requested since this obviously was the key to my arousal, my auditory G-spot, which he fully intended to jab and prod until I succumbed to his manly charms. In fact, the more disgusted I became, the more prolix his obscene tirade. Although he was clearly a native Puerto Rican, he was entirely unschooled in the romantic blandishments of the Latin lover. Rather than whispering in my ear obsequious gallantries, he simply insulted me and praised himself, repeating constantly, "Aren't you a lucky girl? Aren't you a lucky girl to get this FAT PUERTO RICAN COCK?" a rhetorical question to which I gave the obligatory rhetorical answer, in this case (given that I could not speak) a rhetorical mumble, all the while thinking, "Far from being lucky, I am cursed!" At one point, he exceeded even the limits of pornographic hyperbole and had the audacity to say, "You like that twelve-inch Latin COCK, don't you?" a question I could not bring myself to answer since the truth was staring me in the face, a truth some nine inches shy of the oratorical penis he had so eloquently crafted for himself. I finally lost patience when he said, "You enjoy this COCK so much you will give me a few dollars for dinner, won't you?"—a request that, given my sensitivity about those insidious five-dollar bills, I could not take in the same rhetorical spirit with which he had manufactured his massive endowment. Much to his surprise, rage overcame embarrassment, candor prevailed over lies, and after an hour of swallowing my anger, along with my pride (along with his pacifier), I suddenly found my tongue to say, in a voice several octaves lower than my "little voice"—in fact, possibly even an octave lower than my real voice—"NO, I WILL NOT!" He giggled nervously, apologized, and told me he was just kidding, but his remark had dislodged Denial from her wig, garter belt, and "instant face-lift," and Daniel was now in charge and he had taken enough bullshit for one afternoon. I told my trick to cum quickly or I would have to ask him to go, and, much to my great relief, he obeyed and left immediately.

I hate myself for submitting to this kind of extortion. I wish I could say that I caved in out of kindness, out of an unwillingness to hurt him, but the truth is that I caved in out of embarrassment, because I didn't have the courage to transgress the tribal mandate that requires us to maintain peace at whatever cost. Not long ago, I let another stranger into my apartment who had sent me ancient photographs of a young boxer sparring boyishly in front of the camera, a magnificent specimen who, by the time he arrived at my apartment some ten years later, was not nearly as light on his feet—in fact, was at least fifty pounds heavier. We sat and talked for twenty minutes and once again, thinking I could get it over with quickly, I assumed my customary position of subservience, only to stop halfway through and confess that I couldn't go on and that he should leave, which he did somewhat guiltily, without protest, only a few minutes later. The next day, a girl in the room told me that she had met the same man, but rather than inviting him in, she had taken one look at his corpulent body lumbering down the hall, slammed the door in his face, and screamed, "Liar!" I was appalled by her heartlessness at the same time that I envied her frankness and wished that I was capable of reacting so spontaneously, but unfortunately my savoir faire is simply not up to the uncanny predicaments that arise when the phantoms of cyberspace assume a three-dimensional form and materialize on one's doorstep.

Even as I was writing this passage yesterday, a hilarious coincidence occurred. The same girl who had contacted me about her rejection of my boxer sent me an instant message boasting with breathless excitement that an actor from the television program *Oz* was angling for a date, and did I want to see his photograph? After I downloaded the file she sent me, there staring at me from the screen was the ante-Taco-bellum image of my dirty talker. I promptly warned her that this obese braggart was anything but a matinee idol—let alone an actor—as the uninspired delivery of his lines during our afternoon tryst proves, and if he did indeed have a part on *Oz,* it was as the Wicked Witch of the West or, better still, as a Munchkin. We shared a moment of camaraderie, laughing that, although we often seem to be drowning in suitors, there were really only ten men out there on the Internet, ten dexterous Don Juans dashing back and forth between their constantly changing screen names.

I may be a cyber whore who loiters against lampposts in furtive corners of the World Wide Web but I am an old-fashioned girl at heart and even disapprove, to a degree, of Internet cruising, which, while convenient for immobilized shut-ins like myself, is a lousy way to interact with other people. Nothing can take the place of face-to-face encounters. At the very least, one needs to have a brief conversation with prospective partners or even the chance to give them a quick once-over, precautionary measures that prevent overweight men from making unwelcome visits to one's apartment where they ravage you with their phantasmal organs.

Although its rules are bent all of the time, the world of actual physical contact is governed by a strict aesthetic hierarchy in which the beautiful gravitate toward the beautiful. The mediocre and the ugly may gravitate toward the beautiful as well, but the beautiful will most likely gravitate in the other direction, forcing their less-appealing counterparts to settle for other imperfect specimens within their league. The problem with the Internet is that it allows us to do things that reality would never permit us to do; and indeed much of the excitement of online cruising stems from the way we use it to circumvent the laws that govern face-to-face interactions, to appeal to a class of people we could never attract if there were no glass screen between us. These unnatural subversions of the aesthetic order of things would be quite fun if we staged our little insurgencies on our mouse pads, but trouble arises when we insist on dragging our cyber playmates out of the chat room and into the bedroom, where reality intercedes again and restores the hierarchy we fraudulently destabilized by circulating misleading photographs. Not only do we discover that the person we were dallying with is fat and frumpy, but the fat frump discovers that we ourselves do not measure up to the promises of our JPEGs, which, over time, we forget bear only a remote resemblance to us. People are composed of atoms, not pixels, and when pixels coalesce into real matter and knock on doors, or, by the same token, when they open them, the result is often bathos. Constant admiration of our obsolescent photographs, the digitalized Dorian Grays we e-mail hither and yon, leads us to believe that our bodies are much more appealing than they are. Soon we not only deceive others with our retouched, airbrushed, Photoshopped head shots, we deceive *ourselves,* we *become* our JPEGs, forgetting that we are not timeless, are not pixellated bitmaps, psychedelic grids of little squares, but flesh and blood, three-dimensional creatures seen from many different angles—quite a few unflattering—and, what's more, creatures who have changed significantly in the ten to twenty years since the photograph in question was originally taken at one's high-school prom.

The other night I did something I thought I could never bring myself to do: I opened and closed my door in someone's face. A professed actor, he had sent me a glamorous head shot of an athlete in his twenties with a dramatic shock of pitch-black hair; but when he arrived, I peered through my keyhole at a pale graying man now in his late thirties, a shadow of his former self. I had been in a vile state of mind all evening and by the time he arrived I was in no mood to mince words. I opened the door a crack, got a less-obstructed view of the goods, and shook my hand at him in a gesture that said, "Go away, get lost, you lied." I still think back to that gesture with amazement, as if it were not my own hand that had sent him packing but someone else's, the disembodied hand of a heartless fiend. I waved my hand at him as if I were shooing away some pest, as if I were protecting myself from something I was afraid might touch me and that I wanted to keep at arm's length, something that may not have smelled quite right, something unidentifiable yet repellent that one spots in the nick of time just before one steps in it. Granted, I had reason to shake my hand at him and I am glad that I avoided the ordeal of ushering him into my apartment and then ushering him back out again, but I still feel disgusted about the incident, disgusted that I could flutter my fingers so cavalierly, in a way that contradicts everything I've ever believed about courtesy, humanity, empathy. He did an immediate about-face and made his way back to Manhattan, no doubt cursing the lengthy commute he had made to get to my remote Brooklyn neighborhood. I, on the other hand, closed the door feeling, I must admit, along with remorse, a sudden flush of triumph, almost pleased at myself for preventing an encounter that might have ended like the hour I spent with my fat Puerto Rican and his foot-long cock with its missing nine inches.

God didn't let me off so easily, however, and before the evening was over, I was in the arms of someone worse, someone fatter and uglier. Furious and yet still dying for an adventure, I got back online and was contacted by a man without a photograph, an Italian college student who claimed that he was actually talking to me from his laptop in the middle of a lecture he was attending. Although he described himself as a competitive bodybuilder without an ounce of fat, I was unconvinced in light of the ratio of his height to his weight and so, to be cautious, I told him that if he had even a hint of a belly he should tell me now or I would turn him away at the door when he arrived as I had already done one impostor earlier in the evening. He swore up and down that he was in superb physical condition but I reiterated my threat, telling him I was tired of the lying and the bullshit and that, if he were willing to risk it, I would check him out through my keyhole and decide there and then if I would admit him. One peek told me that I had once again been duped, but I was so horny and, what's more, so exhausted by the contempt expressed in the maliciously palsied hand with which I dismissed my first visitor that I let him in. No sooner had he entered than he whipped up his shirt, whacked a very considerable belly, which resounded with a day's worth of snacks from the student-union vending machines, and said, "See, I'm tight as a drum." I found this demonstration, in light of its obvious falsehood, insulting, as if he were not content to trick me but thought so little of me that he was going to rub my face in his deception and even coerce me, through embarrassment, into participating in it. Not surprisingly, we had wretched sex and afterward he apologized for his lack of fervor (not that I was exactly smoldering with lust) and explained, unnecessarily I thought, that he wasn't really attracted to me, that I looked nothing like my photographs, and that he sincerely regretted any disappointment he may have caused with his less-than-impressive performance. If jaws do indeed drop, mine did. Not only was I deceived twice, but I myself was accused of deception by a man who extorted from me complicity in his lie by flaunting his imaginary six-pack, or more appropriately his six-pack*s*, since the heavy consumption of brewskies, along with Dipsy Doodles and Ring Dings, no doubt contributed to the size of his distended belly.

Him

Only a week has passed since my last sojourn into the *New Yorker*'s kennel of Internet dogs, and I now must describe a date with an exotic new thoroughbred. Over the last few months, in response to the many personal ads I have placed, I have received time and time again photographs of a muscle-bound Italian who claims that he has slept with only one cross-dresser, purely by accident, having been deceived by a gorgeous brunette whom he had mistaken for a lanky beauty. At last, after months of flattering e-mail exchanges, we met. The conclusion, of course, was predictable. He was not quite as athletic as he had been when, as a contestant at a bodybuilding championship held well over a decade ago, he had flared his well-oiled lats and flexed his quads for the camera, never suspecting, I imagine, that the photographs of his triumph would end up in the hands of a middle-aged drag queen. By no means was he a ruin of his former self, he was still handsome, he was trim, he had all of his hair, it wasn't gray, but he was most decidedly not the man he had presented himself to be, a towering ectomorph with biceps as taut as steel cables. Having been brazenly deceived time and time again, and having been emboldened by the ugly little trick of the palsied hand, I'm afraid that, perhaps unfairly, I made him pay, not only for his own swindle, but for the swindles of the countless other potbellied slouches who describe themselves as avatars of athleticism. I opened the door, let him in, but stood in the vestibule blocking his passage into the apartment so that I could appraise the goods, which I immediately saw did not pass muster, although the truth is that, had I not seen his purported photographs, I would have been quite content to have sex with him, my refusal stemming solely from the fact that I had been hoodwinked by a man who apparently mistook me for a fool.

I told him that he had misrepresented himself, whereupon he became livid and denied it, claiming "those photographs were taken last October," a whopper that in turn enraged *me,* my eyesight and powers of discernment having been called into question. He insisted on my telling him precisely how he differed from the images he had sent me and so I stated as calmly as possible that I had expected someone who was very "cut up," a man with strong arms and a six-pack, a statement that actually led him to flex his biceps and suck in his belly, as if he were daring me to squeeze the former and poke the latter, an invitation that, in my anger, I accepted, whipping up his T-shirt and gesturing dismissively at his slim but obviously unexercised abdomen. He continued to look at me as if he were in the presence of a madman, someone hallucinating, an inmate of an asylum who mistook a triathlete for an invalid, my wife for a hat, and said quite loudly as he was leaving, "I DON'T FUCKING BELIEVE THIS!!! THANKS FOR WASTING MY FUCKING TIME!!" After I heard the elevator doors close safely behind him, I sat down and wrote him a polite e-mail explaining that I was sorry that I had hurt his feelings but that the photographs he sent me had exceeded their expiration date and that he could expect more rejections—many far more blunt than mine—if he continued to circulate these inaccurate images. To my amazement, a few hours later, he wrote back, telling me again that the photographs had been taken only months ago, that he was in tip-top shape, that "if you found me unattractive turn the lights on and take a good look at me next time," and that—dismayingly—he still wanted me "bad" and would love to meet me again if only I would give him the opportunity to "fuck u like u have never been fucked before."

My mind reels when I think of the depth and complexity of this lie, whose truth he maintained in the face of incontrovertible evidence to the contrary, a fact that suggests that he may not have been in any way conscious that he was deceiving me, that he actually believed he was as muscular as the man in the photographs, a conviction perhaps born of desperate nostalgia for a physique he later told me he had maintained only by taking dangerous quantities of steroids. The mirrors hanging in the cages of the *New Yorker*'s kennel must be fun-house mirrors that permit residents to shed not only pounds, but decades. As I try to understand the psychology of this lie, I even begin to question the evidence of my own eyes, to entertain the possibility that I rushed to hasty judgments, that in my sensitivity to affronts, my anger about being constantly misled, I created an insult to match my already-seething frustrations, imagining a confrontation so that I could prove to myself that I am not a pushover, that I am in control and have the courage to face down someone attempting to take advantage of my goodwill. But even as I begin to feel guilty, my mind returns to those dated photographs and I realize that I am blaming the victim, imagining that I am the one at fault, that I am the one who perpetrated the crime, whereas he tricked *me*. In such a dangerous game of brinkmanship, where guilt becomes a bargaining ploy for sex, the one with the most ticklish conscience always loses. The last thing a polite boy like me expects is that the poor sad-eyed spaniel from the Internet will turn back as it is being booted out the door and begin arguing in its own favor, pleading for affection, begging not to be sent out into the cold, where, it will have you believe, it will be hauled off by a dogcatcher to face almost certain destruction in the municipal crematorium.

I do not want to generalize on the basis of this handful of dishonest men, for I must say that, although the sex I have is usually disappointing, in fact, has been disappointing for much of my adult life, long, long before I put on my first wig, most people do not engage in such gross misrepresentations. While seldom as handsome as they are in their photographs, they are usually trim, young, and masculine, far more than I can legitimately expect given my age and ugliness. Better still, they can be perfectly adorable as human beings, as in the case of the twenty-year-old black football player from East New York who has now visited me some five times, thus making him, out of the dozens and dozens of men who have dropped by (many, I am happy to say, twice), my most steadfast lover. His father named him, unwittingly, after one of the most famous poets in the history of Western literature simply because he liked the sound of the word. When I mentioned to, let us call him, Ovid that he was named after a well-known writer, he smiled and nodded, admitting to me that he had never read the work of his famous namesake, let alone heard of him. He was impressed but not unduly so, the implication being that he was as substantial a man as Ovid and that in some sense, given the absurdly synchronous view of history that characterizes the hip-hop generation, it was more appropriate to say that Ovid had been named after him than vice versa.

Ovid lives with his "granny" in a nearby ghetto, working as a stock clerk as he waits to hear if a New Jersey junior college will award him a football scholarship. His speech is pure Ebonics, his clothing unadulterated rap video, but his manners are as gallant as a courtier's and, while his grandmother may not have introduced him to the pleasures of Augustan poetry, she and, most likely, her church have helped shape a surprisingly refined person who treats me with a gentlemanliness that renders me weak in the knees, eager to make him feel as powerful, as important, as he makes me feel pretty and desirable. Throughout our encounters, he showers me with lewd compliments, telling me how sexy I look, how he loves the way I smell, how he likes me in fishnets, a litany of tender endearments couched in the crudest form of teenage slang, the vernacular of the streets which makes a sentimental liberal like myself burn with ever-brighter ardor.

The feelings I have for Ovid, so tainted by my quixotic leftist idealism, make me question how much lust I really experience during sex, which, rather than expressing desire, expresses something altogether foreign to arousal—namely, gratitude, my thankfulness that he did not run screaming from me when I appeared at the door, that this handsome man with a huge prick and lovely body is sincerely excited by me, that he is able to overlook my imperfections. I am so insecure about my appearance that the person who is capable of relaxing me arouses me and is rewarded with particularly conscientious efforts to please him. I experience desire, not primarily as longing but as a combination of two emotions that one does not typically associate with sex: the relief of self-consciousness and a corresponding pity for my lover, whose own lack of confidence I view it as my duty to allay. In the case of Ovid, pity is inherent in the very nature of the encounter between an educated white man and a poor uneducated black one. I pity him because he comes from the ghetto, because his lack of education portends an unpromising future, because sexual frustration leads him to such an inadequate compromise as Denial, and because I fear that he feels guilty about his bisexual desires. From opposite ends of the world, a white drag queen and a poor black man achieve a racial détente that is as political as it is erotic, a sexual idyll in which two contending tribes lay down their weapons and make love. My bed has become a utopic microcosm of race relations, of ancient hostilities magically overcome in the heat of orgasm. This détente is all the more genuine because the white man, who typically has a distinct advantage in his encounters with black people and is inclined to interact with them with condescending superiority, stands there trembling in his stilettos, pathetically vulnerable and exposed, completely at the mercy of someone who could shatter his self-confidence with the slightest hint of a smirk. The traditionally pitiable person finds himself in the uncharacteristic position of having to extend compassion to the traditionally patronizing one. Even as I write this, I imagine the attacks of my critics, who will quite rightly accuse me of political mawkishness, of a naïve belief in the panacea of sex, but perhaps some will see that there is at least a kernel of genuine emotion here, that I do regret the deplorable state of race relations in this country and that this regret has marked my sexual pastimes, which are not only bestial humpings but social rapprochements. I must not be naïve, however: sex lasts minutes; racism, unlike many of the men I meet, has stamina.

Last night I entertained a handsome Turkish man who, while clearly educated and affluent, raised by globe-trotting parents who shuttled back and forth between London, Paris, and Istanbul, had little of Ovid's finesse. Every few seconds, he would repeat mechanically, like a benediction, "You are my princess" or "You are my girl," slogans he varied with "You are my lady, I am your man," a declaration that almost made me giggle because it instantaneously brought to mind "Me Tarzan, you Jane." "You are so beeyoutiful," he crooned in his thick Turkish accent, and then something that sounded like "I will make you syrupy," but which, after a few repetitions, I finally deciphered as "I will make you so happy." I do not mean to belittle his well-intentioned gallantries, but perhaps because they were so, shall we say, saccharine and conventional, entirely free of the charm of Ovid's gamy street slang, I quickly lost interest in the sex, although I did my best to please him and I am convinced that he was satisfied. Despite his beautiful body and handsome face—far more beautiful and handsome than Ovid's—I was relieved to see him go and I sank down in my recliner and picked up my novel with a renewed sense of the joys of solitude which, in the final analysis, I value far more than the joys of sex.

At one point in my life, I would have leapt at the opportunity of making love with this sort of swarthy heterosexual, but familiarity is breeding not contempt, but boredom. From the moment of

Denial's debut, it was clear to me that my experiment in trans-vestism had a forgone conclusion, that this fantasy would quickly wear thin, that surprise would give way to the inconvenience of a routine whose unremitting monotony no whimsical figment of my self-loathing libido could withstand. What—after all—is the difference between the way a straight man makes love to me and the way a gay man does? The mechanics of sex are identical in both cases. What's more, heterosexuals do not come with brands or tattoos that announce their proclivities in clearly legible letters, nor is it convenient to administer phenobarbital to one's tricks and measure the sweat on their palms with a polygraph as one questions them about their preferences. One must take their sexuality on trust, especially when so few words are exchanged during the encounters and one has so little access to their inner life, experiencing the supposed authenticity of their masculinity solely on the basis of their appearance. Hence, for my purposes, their heterosexuality is largely a moot point and what I get in return for all of my intricate preparations, my corseted discomfort, my compulsive expenditures on cosmetics, my anguish at the failure of my disguise, is exactly the same thing I have been getting all of my life wearing nothing more elaborate—or, for that matter, more costly—than a T-shirt and a pair of white briefs.

I have had a brush with a sociopath, and I am shaken by the experience. Not long ago, I met a good-looking Latino who struck me at the time as stupid as a post, even borderline retarded, so much difficulty did he have in stringing simple words together. On the day after our encounter, my buzzer rang in the late afternoon and in response to my inquiry, the intercom blared the incomprehensible mumbles of my recent visitor, having returned unexpectedly for another go-round. I told him politely that I was not available, that I was sorry but this was not a convenient time; but he was not to be dissuaded and continued stabbing my doorbell with angry insistence. Finally he stopped and I returned to my reading, only to be interrupted minutes later by him pounding violently on the door of my apartment. Through the peephole, I told him again that I was not free but he kept pounding saying, "Let me in," leaving only when, concerned about what my neighbors would think if he continued to make such a racket, I flicked the second lock, put on the chain, and told him that not only was I unavailable but that I was with someone at that very minute and would he please stop bothering me? The following afternoon my doorbell buzzed again, but this time I did not answer it and fortunately no one let him into the building.

The next day, almost like clockwork, the buzzer sounded at 4:00, but this time I called down to the lobby to make my disinterest clear once and for all. Surprisingly, it was not him but Ovid, who asked me if he could come in if he gave me a few minutes to get prepared and I agreed reluctantly, telling him I would use a veil and asking him to return an hour later so that I could at least put on stockings and a dress. At 5:00 sharp, the doorbell rang, and I ushered him into my apartment, darkened by both the drawn blinds and my beaded black veil. He had walked all the way into my living room when to my horror I realized that I had let in the trick from the day before, and not Ovid. Without asking if he could use it, he went into the bathroom and closed the door, whereupon I began surveying the apartment in search of an available weapon, even running into the kitchen and slipping a small carving knife into my garter belt. When he emerged after what seemed like an eternity, he reached out to put his hands on my shoulders but I calmly, and once again with the utmost politeness, told him that "I am going to have to let you go" because my boyfriend was about to arrive any second and that in fact it was he whom I thought I had buzzed in. He shuffled his feet irresolutely, and for a second I was terrified that he would resist, but the specter of an angry boyfriend finally worked and he left without saying a word. Yesterday afternoon, the buzzer rang again, and I expect it will today as well. Granted, such an encounter could have occurred when I was cruising as a man, but coming as it does at the moment I am feeling so exasperated with Denial, it seems like yet another reason for retiring her to my closet.

Her

Her demise seems imminent since I am rapidly losing interest in the disguise itself, in perfecting the mask, a project that has held my interest for months, with every tiny advance and setback causing both delight and dismay. The addictive backstage element of cobbling together my costume and learning the science of state-of-the-art facial prosthetics compelled me to scour the shelves for what cosmetic junkies often call their "HG," their Holy Grail, the product that will make them beautiful overnight. The superstitious belief in the existence of this magical serum is as irrational as the belief in rabbits' feet, but it nonetheless flourishes, in all of its exuberant lunacy, among the sylphs of the makeup counter who entice customers with the promise of instant transformations effected through prohibitively priced creams and gels. I am not a credulous person by nature; my friends, in fact, frequently accuse me of being too wary; but in my desperation to change my appearance, to soften and feminize my craggy features, I swallowed hook, line, and sinker the notion of the occult potion, a bottled, jarred, atomizable transfiguration available, if not at Duane Reade or RiteAid, then at the shops of tonier alchemists like Sephora and Saks. Now, several thousands of dollars later, I have once again become, if not a disbeliever in the miracle of the makeover, then an embittered agnostic who has rent asunder the veil of myths and superstitions that cosmetic companies use in order to keep their customers constantly hunting for the cure. I am obviously not the first person to experience this disillusionment, which has long been the subject of feminist indictments of the beauty industry, but perhaps because I am male, because the challenges I faced were insuperable, and because I did it all within the space of a few months, the trajectory from believer to doubting Thomas has had a kind of illustrative clarity, a swift ascent followed by a dizzying plunge.

Certainly I could learn more about the science of spackling. I could look better than I do. I could refine my techniques, buy better brushes, improve my eyebrows, learn to draw the perfect set of lips; but I now know that, even if I were to begin channeling the late makeup artist Kevyn Aucoin, cosmetician to the stars, I would never look much better than just "okay." Because I have finally explored the horizon of my possibilities, know where they end, having ventured to the absolute margin of my loveliness, I am no longer interested in pursuing an ambition whose conclusion is not only foreordained but anticlimactic. I still buy wigs and I will probably still upon occasion buy makeup (just yesterday I squandered $75 at the new Brooklyn MAC store), but I would really rather spend my money on other aspects of my life that have nothing to do either with my cross-dressing or my sex life, things that will contribute more immediately to my physical pleasure and emotional well-being.

Yesterday after writing the preceding paragraph, I had sex in a way that I have tried only three times, once the other day with Ovid. I had sex as a woman, but without my spackle. The first time I did this was sometime early last year, late at night, after a long, profoundly irritating shift at the law firm where a lawyer half my age had used me like a beast of burden for hours, all the while making curt, critical remarks about the inadequacy of my work. I managed to survive the humiliating ordeal without going into cardiac arrest, as I always fear will happen while I'm being abused by a lawyer; but when I got home, I hit the bottle, got horny, met a man online who lived down the block, and explained to him that, if he were willing to get blown in the dark, I would service him in my wig and stockings, but I would not shave or apply makeup. After he called to tell me that he had arrived in front of my building, I went down to let him in wrapped like a mummy in so many scarves that only my eyes were visible, as if I were wearing some kind of chador—not the most convenient outfit for a blustery night whipped by icy winds. When I opened the door, the scarf around my wig was caught by a blast of air and blown into a bush, and as I was disentangling it from the branches, a second gust tore away the veil covering my stubbly chin, leaving me fully exposed to my gentleman caller, who, taking one look at the bristly hag scrabbling in the bushes before him, muttered a strangled apology, turned abruptly on his heels, and fled off into the night buffeted by the storm. The second time I tried to make love without my makeup, I appeared at the door wearing a veil and a black lace bodysuit which, as my reader may recall, my visitor found so uncanny that he backed away, uttering a horrified "NO!" all but gnawing his knuckle like a doomed teenager in a monster film, only to contact me online a few minutes later to request that I allow him to return but that this time I abandon the costume altogether and dress as a man.

Late yesterday afternoon, one of my regulars contacted me begging for sex and after I explained that I was not dressed and that, handsome as he was, I had no intention of submitting to two hours of preparation for his benefit, I volunteered to have sex in the dark, sans spackle and sans wig. Being horny, he agreed and the encounter went without a hitch—in fact, was unexpectedly pleasurable for both of us, so much so that he returned without warning earlier this evening, foolishly expecting me to welcome him with open arms since my toilette, my customary excuse for not meeting, consisted of nothing more onerous than flicking off a light switch. So this is what I should have done from the start, and in the process spared myself some twelve months of grief: Tell all of my tricks to "pretend" that I am the most beautiful woman in the universe, to close their eyes and fantasize that they are holding Britney Spears or Mena Suvari in their arms, a nubile virgin with creamy white skin as soft as a flower petal and not a forty-six-year-old bald man with hairy armpits and horny yellow toenails. Darkness is the perfect form of drag, shadows the best and least expensive form of makeup. I made a strategic error when I began this project: rather than using a 25-watt bulb, I should have forgone wattage altogether and asked my suitors to bring, along with their condoms, a vivid imagination.

Whither Denial? In the last several weeks, I've been hard-pressed to put on my war paint and greet my public. I simply do not have the energy or interest and although I return from the gym with the best of intentions, determined to experiment with a new way of drawing my eyebrows, blending my blush, or lining my lips, I no sooner shut my front door than I sink into my recliner with a book and a drink and while away the hours until dinner in a state of deliciously studious paralysis, so calm, so relaxed that the prospect of inviting a perfect stranger into this idyll is as appealing as plunging into a cold shower. Denial will not die from shame or bad luck or heartbreak or the sheer implausibility of her disguise but from laziness and inertia, an inglorious end to a plaything that at least temporarily shocked me out of a complacency that once again has me in its clutches.

But it is not simply lethargy that will kill her off. It is the assertion of my old habits, my old self, in short, of the curmudgeonly male who wants to be alone with his art books and novels. Denial will atrophy because her increasingly insubordinate detainee is exhausted by the state of siege in which he has been held hostage for so long, kidnapped by a creature who squanders his free time and burns his money, a wastrel whose habits of procrastination, tipsiness, and thriftlessness have encroached on his former habits of diligence and moderation. Denial will become a casualty, not of outraged masculinity, but of outraged studiousness, not of the man and his machismo, but of the intellectual and his books.

Him

The other evening, out of laziness, I tried the toilette of gloom again and invited a man over for an assignation in the dark. He sent me a photograph of someone whom, under any other circumstances, I would have loved to meet but who lost the contest, hands down, to an even sexier date, a sizzling rendezvous with a paperback novel and a history of Byzantine icon painting. He was obviously in heat and began barraging me with e-mails pleading with me to invite him over, entreaties I ignored until it finally occurred to me that I could try the light-switch trick again and save myself hours of preparation by enshrouding myself in darkness (an option less available to me now that daylight saving time has thrown a wrench into the works and the sun sets long after my customary mating season in the late afternoon). He immediately agreed to my conditions: that I would dress up and wear a wig but no makeup, and that we would make love with the lights off, a prospect he found oddly exciting, titillated by the illicit thrill of screwing a silhouette, a shadow girl whom he could only feel, smell, and hear, sensations I enhanced by spraying myself with copious amounts of perfume and wearing my belly-dancer anklets of tiny jangling bells.

Alas, we had awful sex, and I regretted having agreed to see him, not least of all because, if he could not see me, it stands to reason that I could not see him and thus could not take pleasure in the good looks of a man who, although his face was within inches of mine, his hot breath licking my neck and ears, might just as well have been a noseless leper. Afterward, he interviewed me about my proclivities while sitting on the sofa, with me curled up by his side like an anonymous informer on *60 Minutes,* unseen, lurking in the shadows, speaking with an altered voice, exercising a discretion that it became clear he had misinterpreted from the outset as an expression of coyness, of my desire to remain nameless, rather than simply of the dereliction of my duties as a drag queen.

The encounter was remarkable because my faceless paramour quite openly admitted that it was a failure. In our exchange of e-mails, he became more and more truculent, more rhetorically domineering, until he stated outright that he wanted to stage a mock rape, stressing that I was to be his bitch and that, after forcing me to service him, he was going to throw me unceremoniously facedown on the bed and sodomize me. As soon as he arrived, he began hamming it up, letting his potty mouth runneth over, upbraiding me with insults, which naturally I pretended to find quite wounding to my dignity as a respectable dowager d'un certain age. At one point, for instance, he noticed that I wasn't wearing my heels (I thought that I could safely forgo them in the darkness) and he bellowed at me to "Go put them on, you fucking cunt!" sending me scurrying down the hall, my hands flailing as I flew out of the room, my anklets screaming in protest, as if I had never been so frightened by anyone in all of my life. Unfortunately, he was more insolent than aroused and it was soon clear that neither of us could maintain an erection. Much to his relief, I took advantage of a pause in his tirade and called a cease-fire, whereupon he lunged for his underpants, anxious to put the encounter behind him, as was I. The truth is that, for someone who wears theatrical costumes during sex, I have a surprisingly low threshold for drama in the bedroom and dislike its most declamatory episodes.

No sooner was my would-be rapist partially clothed than Mr.

Hyde subsided into a more amicable Dr. Jekyll, who confessed that the scene had fallen short of his expectations and that he had somehow never felt "in character" but as if he were reading his lines cold, faltering over every word of a bad script. The hectoring bully became a soft-spoken, almost-mousy person. He then proceeded to take his fantasies apart with unsparing candor, laughing at his phony belligerence and his pathetically unconvincing efforts to chastise his disobedient "cunt," a word he admitted he found offensive to women even though he still secretly longed to use it, apologizing to me if I had been put off by his profanities, which of course I wasn't, having been called worse names, and with even greater pleasure, in my day. He said that, whenever he tried to enact his fantasies, reality always intervened and that, although he was aroused by the notion of coercion, he couldn't, as a nice middle-class boy with a college education, conceive of a single occasion in which he might actually have the audacity to bend someone to his will. He was so forthright and self-aware that I suddenly found myself longing to turn on the lights and see this philosopher with my own eyes, but unfortunately the rules of the game mandated complete anonymity, and so we passed like ships in the night, the sounds of distant intelligence reaching across the shadows that divided us.

Her

S ome kind of gang warfare is being waged among the prosti-
tutes in the NYCShemale4male room, a feud between dis-
puting clans that clearly originated offline in one of the bars they
frequent when they are not soliciting (more accurately, belittling
and berating) their Internet johns. In one of the bloodiest of the
battles, the girls began calling each other "low life crackherad[s],"
"2 doll;ar hoe[s]," "dog eating beetches," "low life dog eating
hoes," and "AIDS INFECTED F*GGOT[s]" who wear "stinkin
ass pay less pumps" and are so careless with their hygiene that
they still reek of their last trick. One girl offered to buy another a
bar of deodorant soap so that she could keep herself from
"stanking" but the other politely refused the offer on the grounds
that "U NEED IT MORE THAN ME TO CLEAN UR LOOSE
BOTTY HOLE! UR DRIPPING BOOTY HOLE, U AIDS
INFECTED HO!"

So much for hearts of gold; these girls have toilets for mouths.
The milk of human kindness does not flow from their saline
implants. I think back to an incident that occurred several months
ago, when one of the regular men in the room, a middle-aged
slouch who admits to drinking heavily, reported that he had been
robbed in a Village drag bar during a lap dance in which a buxom
transsexual had bounced up and down on his fat thighs, her rest-
less hands roaming beneath his shirt and into his pants until they

found his back pocket and the several hundred dollars he had so imprudently stashed there. Far from evincing any sympathy, the NYCShemale4male girls laughed in his face and told him that it served him right, that they hoped he had learned his lesson about getting loaded in public, that all johns deserved to be robbed, and that only an idiot would carry that amount of cash in his wallet. The whole incident served to underscore the heartlessness of girls who, in addition to being unkind, are lousy businesswomen, insulting rather than coddling their customers, men so desperate for the privilege of being embraced by these dragons that they turn a blind eye to their glaring flaws, from their cantankerousness to their sticky fingers.

When I watch these on-screen skirmishes, I am reminded of the dark prophecies of left-wing pundits who worried that the lower classes would be excluded from the high-tech revolution but who clearly were not habitués of chat rooms where it would appear that every derelict and drug addict in New York City has a laptop with a high-speed connection. Far from sitting on the curb of the Information Superhighway, the so-called underprivileged are clogging the street, playing bumper cars, a game in which they try to squash each other like roadkill. This great tool of education, this fount of knowledge, this potential experiment in democracy, is not a classroom without walls, it is a gigantic video game without rules. Hand-wringing liberals were wrong to lament the exclusion of the unwashed (and unwired) masses from this new form of self-empowerment, which they idealized as a great leveler of inequalities, as if the second the poor got online they would rush to the Web sites of the *Encyclopedia Britannica* and the *OED* instead of to the sex chat rooms where they have at each other like the Tutsis and Hutus.

One reason these girls are so vicious is that the hormones they take cause PMS, in their case, *Perpetual* Menstrual Syndrome, a state of constant emotional irritability that would seem to be most effectively relieved, not by taking 750 milligrams of ibuprofen and a hot bath, but by picking fights with their rivals and taunting the men who seek their services. One glorious exception to this rule is Maxine, who may be so calm and good-natured because she consumes fewer hormones than most, having been blessed from birth with an androgynous appearance. I became her fast friend when I realized that she is often the only one who giggles (typing "lol," i.e., "laugh out loud," or "lmao," i.e., "laughing my ass off") at all of my stupid jokes, and because I once overheard her asking the room, after I took a brief vacation from cruising, where Silkysatin-desire was, "that nice cross-dresser" who is "so sweet to the other girls." The fact that someone, in a room full of thick-skinned boors, recognized that I am "nice" and try to be compassionate to strangers, even those I cannot see, moved me and suggested a sensibility that, in the context of the moral dim-wittedness of her cohorts, seemed almost exquisite in its refinement.

She tells me that she grew up in an exceptionally tolerant black family that allowed her to dress up as early as play school and stood by her when she began to take hormones in her late teens. Her parents were apparently unruffled when their son became their daughter, as were her siblings when their brother became their sister and her nieces and nephews when their uncle became their aunt. She started seriously entertaining the idea of dressing as a woman full-time when, at the precocious age of fourteen, she began attending ladies' night at a local straight club where she inevitably received four dollars in change whenever she tried to pay the five-dollar entrance fee charged to men. By the time she was in her twenties, she was changing into her uniform in the women's locker room at the food court of a large mall where she worked and never once during the years she held this job did her colleagues suspect that she was a man, even though she did not turn her back to them as she stripped and made little effort to hide the incriminating bulge in her panties. She is so passable that she says that she can wear a woman's bathing suit to the beach and that no one will notice anything awry even when she emerges from the waves sopping wet, the telltale impression of her member plainly in view under the clinging fabric of her bikini.

For one prosperous interlude in her career, she owned a trans-sexual brothel in Queens, work she preferred to her present occupation as a freelance Internet prostitute who charges a modest fee of $150 an hour, a rate that usually translates into $150 for ten minutes since few of her johns stay any longer than this, arriving so keyed up that they cum almost immediately and depart in guilty haste. She tells me she loathes the work and that the men who visit her are all perverted bottoms, "faggits," as she calls them, who ask her to do such things as whip them, pee on them, or even dress them up in women's clothing, like the Chinese businessman who simply wants to hold a conversation with her as he sits at her kitchen table wearing one of her negligees. She says that she must constantly be on the lookout for undercover agents from the vice squad who receive tips from other jealous hookers trolling AOL bent on wiping out the competition, a hazard she has thus far avoided by waiting until her tricks are naked and erect before she asks for money, saying coyly, "Do you have a little something for me?"

She speaks with pride of how she was the first transsexual to break the all-male monopoly held by hustlers on a key part of the Times Square strip—the corner of 42nd Street and Eighth Avenue—where she stationed herself like a menacing black idol and took on all challengers, leading the way for countless she-males and drag queens who soon broke the embargo and turned this intersection into command central for the local gender-bending underworld. To hear her talk about this proud achievement, one might as well be listening to Rosa Parks reminiscing about the role she played in the Montgomery bus boycott and I am somewhat amazed that she would mention this as a genuine accomplishment, much as I might boast that I spent five years in graduate school at Harvard. Certainly, though, within the grand scheme of things, breaking the gender barrier for pre-op hookers at 42nd and Eighth probably exceeds in sheer social impact anything that I myself have achieved in the course of my life, since I have succeeded only in losing a great deal of money with my three books while Maxine's ballsiness actually enabled others to make a living, and quite a comfortable one at that.

She says that in some respects she has always been a prostitute, even during her long romantic relationships, and that she really couldn't imagine affording a man certain intimacies, allowing him to, as she put it, "take pleasure" in her body, without paying for these liberties, if not on a grope-by-grope basis then as her main squeeze, her breadwinner. She seems entirely unaware of the fact that such intimacies work both ways and if she is giving men the rare privilege of touching her, surely they are giving her the rare privilege of touching them, unless, of course, Maxine simply lies still during the nasty parts like some bashful Victorian maiden too ashamed to do anything but play dead until he finishes and she can return to her embroidery. Much as I like Maxine, her attitude toward men is typical of the smug self-confidence that afflicts all of the girls in the room, a confidence bred of the scarcity of she-males, of their exoticism, and of their enormous appeal to heterosexual males. At least some of the bad behavior I witness in the room (Maxine never misbehaves) reflects the malevolent effects of this prima-donna complex. But then perhaps it is understandable that, when they primp and preen before their captive audience, they should play hard to get, the haughty lady, icy and inaccessible, for the truth is that, without their admirers, when they are forced to withstand the scrutiny of the general public out on the streets and not in the chat rooms, their singularity makes them monsters, not goddesses. Their beauty is an acquired taste and while it seems to appeal to a very substantial portion of the male population, their idolaters are still the minority, while the vast majority view them as freaks, grotesque chimeras.

The other night I had the rare privilege of witnessing one grotesque chimera, Bronxcenterfold, meet her match, a girl from

Bushwick who, when she gets into an argument, inevitably gives out her address and asks her enemy to come over and resolve their differences in person. They exchanged the usual vulgarities ("skanky hoe") and bloodcurdling maledictions (an entreaty to God that the other die a lingering death from "ass cancer," AIDS, or, as Da Most Beeyoutiful TS spelled the ethnic blood disease, "Sicko Cell Anima"). They then resorted to an elaborate type of insult in which, having been told by their opponent that they were ugly, they began quoting to the room the flattering comments their suitors were making to them in private, things like "you have beautiful skin," "you have a very sexy look," "mama, you a hot bich," and "baby u look so sexy i would mos def step to u ata club." The strategy seemed so hilarious that I joined in and began posting the remarks—naturally ignored—of a besotted suitor of my own, a man named RICHFOOL, who told me "Silky, I've never seen anyone as gorgeous as you are" and "You are prettier than Pamela Anderson; I want you to be the mother of my sons." Not content to quote the praise they were receiving from anonymous men, they began asking their prospective tricks what they thought of the other girl ("U THINK SHE LOOK BETTER THAN ME OR DOES SHE LOOK LIKE A MONSTER?" and "look very close at the nasty bumps on back of her legs"), gleefully reporting their suitors' responses, "you look better" and indeed "she do look kind a rough there"—an insult that da Bronx countered by saying "clients will say anything for big cox."

Only the next day, Bronxcenterfold, on a psychotic spree of sorts, made the tactical error of attacking Maxine, who marshaled her forces and launched a public critique of da Bronx's physical defects, which are in fact numerous, although she does have a certain plasticine pulchritude. It was open season on everything from her silicone "buttock augmentations" to her wall-eyed breast implants, which Maxine and her Myrmidons said were as supple as granite, at least according to their many shared clients who had giggled in private about da Bronx's myriad deformities. I chimed in that she did indeed look like the Bionic Woman and that she should exercise social responsibility and alter her last will and testament if she had requested cremation, since all of that silicone would almost certainly ignite and cause a chimney fire, creating a plume of toxic ash, a la Bhopal, which might devastate the local flora and fauna, although I doubted that it really mattered since the only other option, burial, would be just as ecologically disastrous, creating yet another Superfund site, which would waste taxpayer dollars.

The incident was unusual in one sense: few girls, unlike Maxine, command enough loyalty that they can enlist the help of their friends when they are fighting for their lives and are lucky if even one courageous soul will step forth in their defense. Although I make a habit of defending perfect strangers, very rarely does anyone put in a kind word for me when my physical flaws are the subject of the lynching du jour. An ally is precisely what one needs in the middle of a catfight, just one person who will remain by one's side so that one doesn't have to face the ill will of the mob alone, a force that loses some of its formidability the second its consensus is called into question. Girls who are fighting are desperate for a helping hand and if a friend should enter the room in the thick of a knock-down-drag-out they call an inexplicably abrupt cease-fire and lavish her with hellos and howareyous, how'syournephews and areyoufeelingbetters, one moment shrieking "skanky hoe beetch!" the next "hi June, hun! Love and kisses, girl!" trying to enlist June's support without coming right out and begging for it. The sociology of fighting in the NYCShemale4male chat room is complicated even further by the fact that the men—the male men, that is—are loose cannons and, in a hateful bid to curry favor, indeed to effect a modest reduction in rates, are often willing to throw their support behind the prettier contestant, thus giving beauty, as in life itself, a distinct moral advantage that it usually doesn't deserve. All it takes is one horny bastard trying to ingratiate himself to some stuck-up queen whose

services he can't afford and one is outmanned, outgunned, transformed into the lone dissident aligned against the hostile mob,
whose acceptance one is desperate to win back, however one
despises its opinion.

I am ashamed that I am so swept up in these petty squabbles, so
obsessed by an activity that is, I think I can say in all due immod-
esty, fundamentally beneath me, too immature for someone of my
advanced years and too abysmally stupid for someone of my intelligence. Life, once so large, has become so small. I have placed
myself at the mercy of savages in their teens, who have turned chat
rooms into the new *Lord of the Flies*. I shiver when I think that it
has come to this, that my heart must survive on the meager crumbs
swept off the table of the Internet, crumbs that contain as much
poison as sustenance. Perhaps I am lucky to have even these scraps
of affection; only eight years ago, still unwired and unplugged, I
would have had neither and my vacuum would have been airtight
rather than peopled with these malcontents whose sadistic antics
create at least the illusion of the laughter and strife of a real social
life. But whenever I am "chatting," my mind constantly harks back
to an image from a play I saw a few years ago, a farce by David
Sedaris whose sister played a chataholic, pounding off messages to
her cyber playmates on an imaginary keyboard, typing with the mad
burlesque glee of the Phantom in *Phantom of the Opera*. The
delirious, commedia dell'arte gestures she made while communi-
cating with far-flung strangers remind me of the preposterousness of
my own social life, which has collapsed into the black hole of unre-
lieved depression.

When the computer goes on the blink, I am deprived of the little
human interaction I manage to scrounge from cyberspace. Two
weeks ago I broke down and purchased a laptop, partly because I
want to watch movies on it and partly because I want to be able to
"chat" in comfort, sprawling in my La-Z-Boy, an act that takes
sedentary cruising to its ultimate twenty-first-century extreme:

supine cruising. With the help of new forms of mobile technology, I am attempting to free myself from my desk chair and meet men in the same position I hope to be in at the end of the evening: on my back. What is the next step, I wonder, in the technological streamlining of romance? "Bot" (i.e., robot) cruising, perhaps? cruising via software programs that fan out across the Web in search of the comely bots of potential mates, exchanging lines of code, like bodily fluids, which specify the type of man I am in the mood for and how low I will permit my standards to sink, that will arrange the rendezvous for me, jostling our complicated schedules, and gently awaken me from my nap when my trick has left his house and is on his way? This change of chairs and positions, from vertical to horizontal, is symbolic of the deterioration of my social life, of my gradual disengagement from other people and, on a larger scale, of the atomization of our entire culture, whose members expend as little energy as possible in their efforts to make contact with each other.

Perhaps the god of conviviality disapproves of this crass reduction of the ancient art of mingling, for naturally my attempts to go wireless have been thwarted by a virus, as well as countless technological snafus that have yet to be resolved. I have been sent to hell for my insubordinate attempts to modernize, indeed, circumvent altogether, the rules of courtship. A simple malfunction of a necessary piece of software led an all-out meltdown of my new laptop and a two-week odyssey into the Kafkaesque world of Dell Computer's and America Online's telephone support. For days now, my agenda has consisted of the following. At 8:00 A.M., I dial a help number and am placed on hold for thirty minutes while a presumably soothing but in fact jarringly loud voice promises that "someone will be with you shortly," repeatedly screaming into the receiver a fabrication that only the most tenacious person can tolerate without hanging up. Once an operator finally answers, I explain my problem and am then directed to the correct department, inevitably the wrong one, as I discover thirty minutes later, by this time suffering full-blown tinnitus after listening to some seventy-five perjurious assurances that "someone will be with you shortly." The new operator politely explains the mistake and in turn sends me on my way to—surprise!—Bangalore, India, where yet another tech-support specialist confesses to me, in an impenetrably thick accent, that he is deeply chagrined—nay, mortified— that he is unable to help me, sending me one step farther up the chain of command, this time to Boise or Houston. From Boise or Houston, I travel back to the subcontinent, being transferred from department to department in a kind of telephonic chain reaction punctuated by interminable interludes of Muzak or a tape that loops between "Your call is important to us" and yet another lie, "Did you know that many of your questions can be answered by visiting our award-winning Web site?"

Each time I am transferred, I feel as if I am getting closer and closer to The Answer, to the solution to my problem, an odyssey that takes on heroic dimensions, becoming an allegorical search for the truth, a quest that leads me through a series of concentric circles like the foyers or lobbies in my own personal hell. I pass from one to the next until I feel that just behind that door ahead, just after the next transfer—my tenth—I will be ushered into the inner sanctum of an all-knowing technological sibyl who will, without hesitation, smilingly part the clouds and intone an ingeniously simple explanation. I can almost hear the hushed rustling of her ceremonial robes, feel the thrill of anticipated release from my dilemma. The last transfer is effected, I take a deep breath, and . . . the line goes dead and a stentorian voice barks out, "If you'd like to make a call, please hang up and try again." As I zigzag through the phone lines from Pretoria to Pondicherry, I feel that I am a hot potato and that the support staff are juggling me along from Peripheral Support to Small Business Sales, their aim being to toss my call to the next operator as quickly as possible before they are burned and forced to expose their ignorance. After I hang up, I collapse in my recliner, overcome with a keen sense of nihilism, an overwhelming conviction that the world has stopped working, that order is breaking down, things falling apart, the machines around us sliding into disrepair, our world gradually taking on the obsolescent appearance of a cinematic dystopia. And the cause of this chaos: one man's unwillingness to sit upright while he flirts.

Perhaps it is appropriate that I end Denial's saga on this apocalyptic note. She is the product, after all, of Internet atomization and would never have existed in the days before take-out sex, before lusty—albeit lazy—solipsists met their paramours via the futuristic procuress of a popular home appliance. Others experience existential crises when a parent dies or a child leaves home or a job ends unexpectedly; I have experienced mine after a more banal, electronic calamity, the result of a bad habit that I avoid scrupulously with the men I meet: unprotected sex with another computer.

Epilogue

A s I write this, my eyes return again and again to an unsightly patch of skin on my lower abdomen. I have not shaved my body for weeks, and my hair is growing back. Coarse tufts are sprouting like whiskers out of moles and circling my belly button like a sparse, ratty fringe. It has taken only two years of more-or-less constant shaving for me to grow accustomed to my feminized skin's sleek, baby-butt baldness, and now I recoil from the sight of these bristly filaments, which seem to belong to another body. There is hair on the back of my hands and on each of my toes, on the first joint of my fingers and the pink brown areolas around my nipples. There is hair on my knees and hair on my elbows. My eyebrows are regaining their former unkempt lushness. Denial is disappearing beneath a jungle of hair follicles like an Aztec temple beneath the creeping vines of a Mexican forest.

Inertia did her in, inertia coupled with sobriety and thrift. Denial was in large part the creation of booze and money. The three drinks I had during my 4:00–6:00 P.M. happy hour gave me the courage to do things that I probably wouldn't have done stone cold sober—or, more accurately, gave me the energy, not the courage, since I usually do not have to contend with shame but with laziness and dysphoria, forces that inhibit my behavior far more than mere cowardice. In an effort to control my depression, I have ceased drinking almost entirely and so I have lost the liquid propellant that gave me the vigor both to do my makeup and undergo a costume change that, once it lost its novelty, became an outright chore, an irksome task I found myself postponing, tormented by procrastination, by tactics of delay that seemed odd given that what I was deferring was something that few people, when given the choice, are willing to postpone: sex.

At the same time I abandoned my beloved three cocktails, I was forced to find a new job and, having taken a substantial cut in pay, no longer had the disposable income I once threw into this former sinkhole in my budget, a cash drain that, at the height of Denial's prodigality, was siphoning off as much as $100–$150 a week. Denial was sustained by her purchases. She was a figment of a consumerist imagination, kept alive by shopping, with each strategic acquisition providing a new chapter, a new discovery, an improvement in the look, an advance in my mastery of the craft. When I slashed and finally curtailed her budget altogether, there was nothing to look forward to, no blowout sale of whorish hosiery, no lip glosses with "advanced optical technology," no "scientifically engineered" mascaras that allow you to "take control of your lashes." The spirit of giddy experiment was gone from the project forever, and although I still have enough lipsticks and eyeshadows to do my makeup for at least the next decade, they are the same lipsticks and eyeshadows, and they hold no surprises.

It wasn't simply that I could no longer afford Denial: I no longer believed in the possibility of her improvement. Once I lost faith in the HG, the Holy Grail, the miracle cure for my ugliness, there was simply no need to continue rummaging the shelves of Sephora in search of some overlooked scientific breakthrough that would revolutionize my appearance. Trying out new blushes and eyebrow gels was an enterprise whose conclusion was pathetically forgone.

What's more, I became convinced that Denial, the whore, was actually dangerous for Daniel, the hermit. The last thing a man who spends five days a week working in almost-total solitude needs is more excuses not to leave his apartment. My promiscuity has always been a way of compensating for my lack of social opportunities, but Denial, who gives new meaning to the word "homebody," limited my opportunities even more drastically, returning me to the closet in a sense, to a secrecy that I had long since abandoned, having come out to my parents at the age of thirteen. I do not want to go back into the closet, don't want to hide from my neighbors, feel guilt about dragging my filth into a respectable middle-class apartment complex crawling with children. Being a cyber slut has effectively thrown me back into the pre-Stonewall era, where my love life is the subject of constant burning shame. As a homosexual who has always prided himself on his openness, such a reversion to subterfuge represents an intolerable state of affairs and one that has the unfortunate consequence of reinforcing my agoraphobia. At least when I cruised out of doors, I took recreational strolls in the park; but when I cruise as the cartoon cur in *The New Yorker,* I am tethered to my keyboard.

Will I miss her? Worse, will I look back at the Denial chapter in my life with embarrassment, mortified that I could play such silly games at such an undignified age? To protect myself, I rely on a belief I have always held, that the self-aware are never truly pathetic, that their panoramic vision of themselves and their relations to others redeems them, and that only those who have no sense of how they are perceived by their society truly merit pity. Only those who are not laughing can be laughed at, and there can be no doubt that Denial, even during the worst of her humiliations, bore on her face, if not the idiotic grin of hilarity, then the thin glaze of an archaic smile.